MW01077392

Trans Parent Diary

The Story of My Transition
When My Daughter Became My Son

By Karen Lander

Copyright © 2021 by Karen Lander

All rights reserved. No part of this publication may be reproduced or transmitted, in any form or by any means, without written permission of the copyright owner except for the use of quotations in a citation.

To request permission, contact the publisher at:
        publisher@innerpeacepress.com

ISBN: 978-1-7351738-1-8

Trans Parent Diary: The Story of My Transition When My Daughter Became My Son

Initial paperback edition, March 2021

Published by Inner Peace Press
Eau Claire, Wisconsin, USA
www.innerpeacepress.com

Gratitude

Thank you, Pat, Myrna, Bernadine, Corina, Debbie, Ben, Alicia, Nicole, Patricia, Corey, Cheri, and Heather for your support, input, suggestions, ideas, and encouragement as I moved along this writing journey.

Thank you, Alex, for being OK with me sharing our story with the intention of helping others, and for still helping me when I get stuck on life's journey.

Cover design by Debbie Stratton at Design Dog Studio

Corinthians 13: 4-7

Love is very patient and kind, never jealous or envious, never boastful or proud, never haughty or selfish or rude. Love does not demand its own way. It is not irritable or touchy. It does not hold grudges and will hardly even notice when others do it wrong. It is never glad about injustice, but rejoices whenever truth wins out. If you love someone you will be loyal to him no matter what the cost. You will always believe in him, always expect the best of him, and always stand your ground in defending him.

- Holy Bible, New King James Version (still a best seller)

TABLE OF CONTENTS

Introduction

I HAVE A TRANSGENDER TEENAGER

I have a transgender teenager.

This means the daughter to whom I gave birth seventeen years ago identifies as a boy.

He dresses as a boy and wears his hair short. We legally changed his gender, first with a simple signature on a permission form from his school district, then legally on his birth certificate and driver's license. Because of the testosterone he injects into his abdomen every Tuesday, he sports typical hair on his legs, under his arms, and on his face, and he has an Adam's apple on his neck. He had the excess flesh on his chest surgically removed so that it is flat, and he wears a silicone penis in his briefs.

My son also often paints his nails different colors, including blue and red. His fingers and wrists are adorned with bracelets and rings he's made himself. He cuts and colors his own hair, and typically wears it in a very cool mullet, short on the sides and long on top (it looks awesome – really). It's usually a different, bright and beautiful color – pink, blue, purple, or green.

He knows who he is, what he likes, and what makes him feel authentic. He has no tolerance for fake people and very little patience for people who are unwilling to face the facts of their lives.

I am the mother of a seventeen year old transgender boy named Alex.

My child, who used to be named Leah, is now named Alex. His driver's license and social security card both say so. I never had a clue that Alex saw himself as a boy rather than his physiological female assignment until he told me. This happened when he was thirteen years old. He had been a happy little girl, a typical, ordinary, normal little girl who played with dolls, went to sleepovers, and made friends easily. Leah always had a couple of boys wrapped around her little fingers. She was a lover of everyone.

Alex is a happy young man. He is a leader at school and has sincere and fun friends. His hobbies include hanging out with his younger brother, playing the trombone, lovin' on his puppies, decorating and redecorating his room, reading, painting, making jewelry, and drawing. He relishes time with friends, but also cherishes time alone. He is an empathetic and caring darling. He is incredibly understanding and compassionate with people who are trying to be real, whether they are kids his age or adults. He's been like this since he was very young.

Learning to be a good parent took a lot of adjusting on my part. I was a teenager in the 1970s. That was a different era. Kids were taught to do what they were told. We were not encouraged to seek our authenticity; that didn't even mean anything back then. I was the child of parents who themselves were not authentic or evolved. My mother suffered from mental and emotional illnesses that I tiptoed around, and my dad was very self-centered and truly only concerned with what made him happy. My brother and I were given food, clothing, and shelter, but were in no way taught how to navigate life so we would be successful adults, and we were discouraged from identifying, let alone pursuing, our dreams.

I was raised to shut off my emotions. I learned I was supposed to stay out of my parents' way and not ask for anything more than what was already being given. I learned that I shouldn't expect anything, because then I wouldn't be disappointed. Growing up in this kind of environment caused a lot of emotional damage that has taken both my brother and me our whole adult lives to overcome.

And so, when my child started to change how he identified himself and started asking to be treated differently, I didn't have a clue, let alone any skills, to know how to respond. If it had been me, my dad would have told me my idea was stupid and that it was never going to happen. I would have known not to ask my mother. I was sad and scared and mad that I didn't know how to be Alex's mother.

I knew that it was important to listen to my child, and that I needed to support her (or his?) transition, but I honestly didn't know how to do that. I didn't know how to show I cared. I didn't know how to get involved, to advocate for, and to investigate on behalf of. I just knew what my parents would have done with my ideas: ignore, deny, and ridicule. And I knew I couldn't do that to my child.

So, I had to figure out how to be a good parent. I had to transition my ideas, habits, and expectations for being *her* mom to being *his* mom, and I had to learn what I hadn't been taught by my parents. My world had to change as much as his, and with that came a more evolved and deeper love for both of my children.

I am the mother of an outstanding human being who is going to live happily ever after.

My transition taught me what my parents didn't: I learned that healthy parental love means giving both of my children direction, experiences, empathy, and encouragement so they will evolve into the humans they came here to be. They aren't a mistake. They, like each of us, have a reason for being here. Love doesn't mean letting them do whatever they want, or conversely, hovering over them like a helicopter so they don't grow.

When my child started to become someone different than I was expecting, I learned to identify my feelings – and there were a lot of them! I realized the thing that was hurting the most was that I was grieving the loss of my daughter. I recognized I was going through the various emotional stages of grief.

In 1969, a psychiatrist named Elisabeth Kübler-Ross, who worked with terminally ill patients, wrote a book called *On Death and Dying*. I still had this book on my bookshelf from graduate school, and I pulled it down and opened it up.

There are five emotions that Kübler-Ross's patients went through as they came to terms with their impending death.

> These stages include:
> 1. Denial (including shock and fear)
> 2. Anger
> 3. Bargaining
> 4. Depression
> 5. Acceptance

Though Kübler-Ross's model of grieving has been revised over time, the original idea accurately describes the journey of emotions that I experienced as my daughter started becoming my son. Remembering the stages of grief helped validate and organize my feelings.

Nobody goes through these stages one to the next, which means people's feelings and emotions fly all around, like a kite high in the windy sky. I was no different. Like a lost tourist in an unfamiliar city, I wandered back and forth, up and down, and around and around and around these various stages of grief.

As parents, our purpose – our assignment – is to love our children, and it might come as a complete surprise and be utterly shocking when we're confronted with the unexpected. When they change in a way we weren't planning for, hoping for, grooming them to be, it's perfectly normal to wonder, "what does that mean? How can it be less scary? What if we don't know what to do?"

With the help of a mother of one of my child's friends (who also has a transgender son), and a very patient and insightful counselor, I realized that I wasn't going to lose my child because she thought she was a boy. But that's exactly how I was feeling. They reminded me that I would always have the memories of her. More importantly, though, I would have a relationship with my child. And if I could accept and embrace him as he was becoming and how he was seeing himself, he would feel safe to share with me his continual evolution and transformation. Most importantly, we would have new experiences and make more memories, and he would be happy.

This one thought gave me peace: I wasn't losing my child.

Why This Book?

I wrote this book with the hope it will help other parents who are struggling with the new idea and progressing reality that their child is different than she or he used to be. Everything in this book is true and happened, though some of the situations have been condensed or combined. And just so you know, I have changed every name (including mine) in this story for protection and confidentiality.

The first three chapters introduce you to me, and you'll learn my story and hopefully understand what made this transition – my transition – so difficult. I had "issues." (News flash: we all do!) I had to acknowledge, face, and deal with my "issues" in order to get to a place of peace. You'll also be introduced to who Alex was when he was Leah, and you'll meet a little bit of Nate, Alex's younger brother.

The next five chapters are organized according to the five stages of grieving and include personal stories that correspond to each stage. Though the chapters are in order of Kübler-Ross's line, the stories themselves aren't chronological or in any sort of order. I hope this doesn't confuse you.

Alex's story, in his own words, is included, as well as the definitions of new words Alex gave me when his transition began. These are terms that are important to know. I've also included a page of a few of the many resources available to help you and your child when your child wants to make a major life change like mine did.

And finally, at the end of the book is a journal called "Just One Thing." It's included so you have safe space to release your thoughts and feelings. I've added different prompts to help you document the journey. I wish I would have had a format like this to follow; I'm sure it would have helped me calm down and remember what was most important. I encourage you to make notes in the journal or keep your own special separate journal. Please be sure to write the date of your entries and return to each prompt multiple times. You may be surprised at how your thoughts and feelings transition as time passes. Journaling heals the heart and clarifies the mind, and it's important to keep a sound heart and mind.

However you travel on this journey with your child, and whatever you think and feel, I encourage you above all to be patient, kind, and loving equally to your child and with yourself. Time will pass, and things will work out, if you'll remember that your child needs your love and acceptance more than anything.

It is not an accident, but rather by supernatural design, that you and your child are in each other's lives. You are together to help each other grow.

Be strong and of a good courage,
Karen

I Am Who I Am

THE STORY OF MY LIFE

On the outside, I look normal.

I have been divorced twice and am now married to my soul mate, Chuck. (Third time's a charm. I'm his second wife. Lucky guy.) Together, we are raising my two teenagers, who I created with my second husband. We have our own business, a home, two dogs, investments, an RV, good credit scores, and three cars (since one of the kids drives). We live in the suburbs of Denver, Colorado. It's 2020 (now 2021) and the whole world is living in the twilight zone of a global pandemic. It's a wonderful life.

On the inside, in my own head, I'm not normal.

I have always felt different from everyone. Maybe it was because I was adopted at birth. I always knew I was adopted, and I knew my younger brother, Bryce, was also adopted. My adopted mother had told me that she had a very difficult time bonding with me when I was an infant and barely held or touched me for the first several months of my life. One counselor suggested that this was a form of abuse and explains my inability to trust myself, people, the world, the future, life. Apparently, I suffer from a condition called Reactive Attachment Disorder.

MY CHILDHOOD

I was raised in a small town in Wyoming. When I was old enough to understand, I realized my adopted mom was sad. Something made her hit me or slam my head on things when I did something wrong, and I instinctively knew it wasn't just because she didn't take her thyroid pill or that she was too tired from running a daycare center by herself, keeping our giant house clean, and always having a hot meal on the table for dinner. It was our little secret, though, this inappropriate and over-the-top violence towards her little girl who did things like stay at a friend's house for lunch instead of coming home. She never taught me how to shave my legs, or what was happening when I got my period. When I was about ten, she looked at me one day and said, "you know, Karen, when you grow up, you're gonna be really ugly." It took me until I was in my late forties before I decided she was wrong. I found out later what made her sad, and this helped me understand her behavior and forgive everything she'd done to me.

On the other hand, my adopted dad was a controlling, uncaring, textbook narcissist, though back then, there were no readily available textbooks on this topic and other mental health issues. Like my mom and I did, he and I also had a little secret: it was a game we sometimes played, like at dinner, or at a restaurant, or in the car driving to visit grandparents two states away. He would first form a zero with his fingers by curling his fingers and thumb of one hand together. Then he would squeeze his hand into a fist. Then he would point up with his thumb, keeping his fingers together. It was code for:

Oh.

Shut.

Up.

From this, I learned to keep my thoughts and ideas and opinions to myself, because, well, nobody wanted to hear what I had to say. My thoughts and ideas were obviously ridiculous so would I please not embarrass him or myself with my foolish notions. I didn't realize – and probably he didn't either – how damaging this was to me.

Like when I was eleven. I got this insane idea that I wanted to write a book about the interesting people in my little town. So for Christmas that year, I asked for a typewriter and tape recorder so I could get started. But how could I possibly know what I wanted? So my parents got me an electric blanket instead. Parents know best, right?

We went to church for a few years when I was in grade school, and I found the Sunday School lessons comforting. I liked the boundaries that Christianity offered, especially the 10 Commandments – the Top 10 as I called them long before David Letterman coined that phrase. I honored my parents as best I could, because I didn't know that what was happening wasn't right. I just felt like it was the right thing to do.

I wasn't protected or supported, encouraged or loved, and I have often wondered why I was adopted by these people. They didn't really seem to want me or my brother. Growing up in a dysfunctional home in the 1970s was not what it is like today: teachers and school counselors hadn't yet learned to notice signs of depression and neglect stemming from issues at home.

When I was in junior high, I spent a lot of time alone. We had moved from the safe, little town in Wyoming to a large city in Colorado. Here, I started junior high school with a class of strangers who were prettier, wealthier, better dressed, and cooler than I would ever be, and I had an impossible time fitting in.

My brother and I were left on our own, as both my parents worked, so we came home to an empty house and hid in our bedrooms. I spent day after day being bullied by the boys and taunted by the girl, and had no one to talk to about it. I don't recall either parent ever asking or even particularly caring how my day went.

I discovered thrift stores and used bookstores and was drawn to books written by Norman Vincent Peele, Catherine Ponder, Robert Schuller, Napoleon Hill, and Leo Buscaglia. I loved reading the messages about living with enthusiasm, thinking positively, believing in a higher power, taking control of my thoughts, and being and giving love. These were good ideas, but I had the darndest time accepting that they were meant for me. They were meant for everyone else – the important people, the people who mattered, those who belonged. I liked reading the good ideas; I just wasn't good enough for them to apply to me.

Neither parent helped my brother or me develop and grow, let alone to get ready to be an adult. Neither cared about our dreams nor helped us set goals. For some crazy reason, my mom refused to let me take home economics in junior high, yet she didn't teach me how to cook. My dad was a businessman and a hospital administrator, and yet his career advice was for me to be a teacher. I had already started my own little business at the age of thirteen, yet "teacher" was his recommendation. Not "business owner" or "writer" or "manager." (I don't think he would have known the word "entrepreneur," but that's what I became.)

I finally made a few friends, and we all had secrets, too. None of us talked about our situations, including that one time when a friend and I were walking home from junior high school and when we got to my home, we saw an ambulance with its lights on, parked in my driveway. My friend started to panic, and I nonchalantly replied, "oh that's just for my mom. She must have tried to kill herself again."

And we continued on to her house.

This was my life: coming home from school and

checking my parent's bathroom to see if my mom had hanged herself.

These were normal, typical days.

Because my poor mom had tried to kill herself before.

We never talked about it as a family, or to one another, or to anyone. Nobody got any medical or mental help.

Once I was nearly done with high school, I started to see my life and situation for what it was. I was on my own, and if I wanted to do anything with my life, I had to figure it out on my own. Nobody I knew had walked in my shoes and dealt with the things I had dealt with. And just like Leah did years later, I learned to do things that worked for me. Once I figured this out, there was no turning back. So in a way, my parents did prepare me for the life I have lived.

Maybe I have felt different because I am different.

AFTER HIGH SCHOOL

I made it to graduation, then left home and went to college (paid for by myself, plus I miraculously got some scholarships). I attended a women's college in Missouri. I met other students whose parents believed in them. Wrote to them. Sent them money and care packages. Supported their dreams of being an artist, or a broadcast journalist, or an archeologist, or a pilot, or a whatever. Their parents said things like, "Oh, let me introduce you to this person. They'll help you. They'll teach you. Oh, and here's some money to get you started."

Help? Support? That would have been so nice. I had uncles and aunts and cousins with money and influence, but nobody offered to help.

Because of how I was raised, and because I knew what it felt like to not be accepted or encouraged, and to not feel safe, protected, and supported, I didn't know how to date or have healthy, good relationships with men. And I never wanted kids. I could barely handle myself, honestly. I married the first guy who showed any interest in me. He had a juvenile prison record, but he was really nice. We divorced two years after getting married, and after I'd miscarried a baby at twenty-two weeks. Baby Phillip was fully grown on the outside, with a full head of hair, ten perfect little fingers and toes. And I think he knew I wasn't ready to be a mommy.

It wasn't until I realized I was happy I'd lost this baby that I accepted the idea that I wasn't healthy or normal or happy. I started getting counseling and attending Al-anon meetings, and after several years, I found a great church that taught all about a God, who some called "Father," and this Guy loved me unconditionally. I was the apple of His eye. Wow – quite different from the earthly father I got. This relationship with God became another secret, and the one I cherished most. I heard from Him. I was guided by Him. I was protected and inspired by Him. I heard His still, small Voice all the time. He has never left me and is with me still today, even when I don't listen or take any interest in His ideas.

When I was in my mid-thirties, I started a business and was happy, growing, and learning about myself. I started attending a different church, where they taught about the Jewish roots of Jesus. Something hit me at my soul's level; it made so much sense. Was I Jewish? I ordered a DNA test online and a few weeks later, I learned my ancestors came from a small area in Eastern Europe that was predominately Ashkenazi Jewish.

Then, another thing happened. I met a man at this new church, and I knew he and I would have wonderful children.

I thought to myself, *Say what? KIDS? I don't want kids!*

"Trust me," said that still, small Voice of God.

Scott and I were married six months after meeting, and within three years, we had produced two amazing kids.

MARRIAGE AND BABIES

My first born was Leah. My darling daughter. She was so cute, with curly brown hair, and a sparkling personality. She had a look and an essence about her that people have noticed and commented on her whole life, and she could heal a broken heart with her smile. Leah was inventive, curious, and fearless. She had a boyfriend as soon as she started preschool and had a group of girlfriends who played and dreamed together. Smart as a whip, she pretty much taught herself how to read when she was about three years old, and she often answered questions out loud that I was thinking to myself.

My younger child, born two years and two months after Leah, was Nate. When he was a toddler, we called him Nate-zilla because he would crawl over to Leah's blocks and knock them over. He has a twinkle in his eye even to this day. He is loyal, sensitive, inquisitive, and as handsome as they come. He has always been able to remember things, including phone numbers, addresses, and commercials. When he was in preschool, we all remember him impressing the fireman who came to the Parents' Day BBQ when he quickly and correctly recited the phone numbers of my work, my cell, the preschool hotline, and the entire scripts of different TV and radio ads, including Frank Azar and the Shane Company (both local businesses).

My children have always been best friends. They are both very bright and funny. They learned early in their lives to lean on and share with each other. We have always been close, and I'm so grateful for this.

Marriage to their father was a different story. It didn't take long for us to realize our incompatibility in every component of a marriage, and if it had not been for the kids, I think – no, I know – our marriage would have ended much earlier. But, when they came along he was loving and doting to them. He taught them how to say "Abba" as their first word (it's a Hebrew word that means "Father"). He also taught them how to count in various languages, including Japanese, Russian, and Hebrew, and how not to be afraid of trying new things. He didn't like following rules, so he didn't teach them things like appropriate bedtime, the importance of brushing their teeth, and why they should do their chores.

Scott and I differed on the basics of everything. I learned very quickly NOT to disagree with him. His ideas were all that mattered, and he was going to get his way regardless, because my opinions and needs did not matter at all. I'd lived this way my whole life, so I easily went along, though it troubled me inside. Scott had no problem inflicting emotional or physical power over me, so I learned to keep quiet and let him have his way. It was just easier. Like it was with my dad.

One night, I was in the kitchen, alone, doing the dishes, thinking about the state of my life and the potential future I would have. Scott was out of town for work (he had a job repairing lasers in medical offices and travelled across the western states), probably getting too drunk, spending too much money, and hooking up with a stranger for the night. All things he did almost every time he was on the road.

We had recently started a new business that I conceived. It was a medical spa that specialized in laser hair removal, which, back then, in 2006, wasn't something most people knew about. (This was before Groupon and Google. Long, long ago....) Within a week of opening the doors, I knew it was a mistake to have started a business that relied on his expertise. When he wasn't traveling, he worked in the spa. He didn't know how to talk with clients, make sales, or market, but he did have three specialities: operating the laser, spending money we didn't have and hadn't budgeted for, and downloading pornography from the Dark Web.

As I stood by the sink, drying dishes, I was considering my options. There was too much debt, too little money, a bankruptcy, and a federal tax lien. Scott didn't care. He was a drunk, I had learned too late, and a mean one at that. In his opinion, I talked too much, had stupid ideas, and was a bitch. I was scared to death of this man. He was a bully. Mean. Hostile. Intimidating. Emotionally and verbally angry. I felt trapped.

Leaning over the sink, I started crying, realizing my impossible predicament. Leah came into the kitchen and, in her little four-year-old voice, asked, "why are you crying Mommy?"

I was startled by her. I looked up at her, my darling daughter, in her favorite pink bunny jammies, a toddler size onesie with the feet sewn on, plus bunny ears and a little white, round cotton tail. Her curly hair was still a bit damp from the bath she had been given earlier, though I'd put her and Nate to bed an hour ago.

Without thinking, I answered, "I think I need to divorce Daddy."

And then something extraordinary happened. Leah looked at me with her soulful eyes, full of wisdom and a deep knowing that came from ages ago. She looked deep into my eyes and quietly said, "not yet Mommy."

I stopped drying dishes.

Leah walked over to the couch and climbed up on the arm rest. Without thinking, I joined her in the living room and automatically sat down on the floor, at the feet of Leah. Leah crossed her little bunny legs, interlaced her little fingers then wrapped them around her knee.

"Mommy," she began, "it's not time to leave. We have to stay here in this house for a little while longer until the Voice says we can go."

"What voice are you talking about?" I asked, tears swelling up in my eyes.

"You know what the Voice is Mommy. It talks to me. It's the same Voice that talks to you."

I was stunned. I'd forgotten about that Voice. I sat up straight.

"How does your Voice talk to you honey?"

Leah smiled. I noticed her face looked radiant, like a spotlight was shining on her. Her eyes were dancing, and her voice sounded different, like someone else, someone older, was speaking.

"Mommy. My Voice is in my heart and my brain.

I just know. Like when someone is sad or mad. Or when someone is gonna get sick. And I see a light around them, or sometimes I see a shadow. Like around Daddy. He has a shadow around him. I don't like it."

"Have you always seen these things and the shadow?"

"Can I tell you a secret, Mommy?"

I nodded, wiping my face, which was wet with tears.

"I heard the Voice before I got borned."

I gasped.

"What do you mean?" I whispered.

"I always heard you and daddy talking to me. I heard you singing to me. And I heard you crying when Daddy said kinda mean things to you. And then I always heard a different Voice that told me I was getting borned to help you."

I was stunned and didn't know how to respond. This was my little girl telling me things she couldn't have known.

"You and Daddy had to get married so you could make me. I had to be borned. I have important things to do to help people."

"How do you know this?" I asked, stunned.

"The Voice told me. The Voice talks to all of us."

I shook my head, trying to clear my thoughts, which were tumbling over themselves.

"Does Daddy hear the Voice?" I asked.

"Not anymore Mommy. He's too sad. He only has a shadow on him now."

"Can we help him?"

Leah frowned and shook her head. "I don't think so Mommy. But we can't leave yet. We have to stay a little while longer."

"Is the Voice telling you this?"

"Yes."

"Does your Voice know when we can leave?"

Leah looked deep into my eyes, which were leaking tears. "You have to ask your Voice again, Mommy."

I looked at Leah. There was a glow around her body, seemingly flowing through her, and it was not the light from the floor lamp. The hairs on the back of my neck and my arms sprang up, and I got goosebumps.

Breathing deeply, I calmed down and wiped my face with my sleeve. Though she was so young, my little girl was obviously aware of the stresses between her dad and me. More profound, though, was that she knew what and how to say what I needed to hear. Something supernatural was happening. Leah was speaking with the wisdom of an old, wise soul, telling me exactly what I needed to know. The Voice was speaking through her to me.

A few weeks later, I woke up after a night of fighting with Scott. I had reconnected with my Voice, and that morning, I heard the message I was waiting for.

It was time to go.

Leah saw me packing and smiled. "I heard it too Mommy." She got her suitcase out of her closet and began to pack her stuffed animals then helped Nate pack up his toys. We left that day, the three of us. A friend had agreed to let us rent their spare bedroom for ninety days.

Onward and upward with my precious Nate-zilla and Leah, the old soul.

We are on the way to a better life,
where all our needs are met.

Single White Female

IT GETS BETTER

Once we got settled, I headed to an affordable hair salon for a cut and color. I'd grown my hair long and dyed it blond for Scott, thinking/hoping it would make him like me, tolerate me, accept me, or love me maybe just a little. Here's some free advice: never bleach your hair blond for a man. It turns your hair – and your heart – into straw.

This was the beginning of my new life, and I was scared to death. Here I was – a single mom to two little chickens (my nickname for them) under the age of four. I had no money, no family, and no friends (our few friends sided with my ex-husband). I also had a nine-month-old baby business that I had created out of thin air with Scott's input. When I left him, I had monthly operating expenses of $30,000. That was $1,000 a day that I needed to make in a business that was brand new and very fragile.

I also had no credit. Two years prior, I'd had to file bankruptcy. (Scott had no credit, and I learned not to say "no" to him. I paid the bills and kept a job, but he always outspent.) I also had a $10,000 tax lien. Here's some more free advice: when the IRS sends you a letter saying they want to audit you, don't listen to your sociopathic husband who insists you ignore those stupid letters and annoying phone calls, because the government can't do anything. Guess what? They can. And they will. And they did. I had that federal tax lien on my credit report for ten years, which prevented me from getting any credit for an entire decade, which just made everything that much harder.

But that wasn't all. Next up: the 2008 recession crashed the economy, which meant that people stopped spending money except on the bare necessities. And I didn't offer a necessity. All around me, card shops, clothings stores, and import businesses closed their doors for good in the middle of the night; often, the owners just walked away.

I didn't think quitting was an option for me. After all, I didn't have anything or anyone to fall back on. As the bills kept coming, I fell behind on many of my payments. It was humiliating to contact the companies and ask for mercy and extensions.

I thought that leaving the crazy man would make things easier. Not being able to pay bills was another personal failure that haunted me. I felt like such a loser. I was depressed, sad, embarrassed, and very alone. I was mostly very, very scared (terrified, really) and completely stressed.

Being an adult child of an alcoholic mother and a disinterested father had programmed me to be independent and self-reliant. I was on my own, and nobody was going to help. I wasn't taught how to have dreams and set goals to accomplish them, yet I still managed to keep moving forward. So walking away from this business wasn't an option. I was almost like a robot; quitting did not compute. I had no secure foundation, and nobody or nothing to fall back on or help me up if I fell, so I had to make this business – and my life – work. I had so many fears about so many things:

- I was going to lose my business, which would mean no source of income. This real fear of no money and lots of debt was debilitating.
- I wouldn't be able to pay my rent for my business, so I would be mocked and scorned by the remaining tenants in the mall where my business was, and I would be so ashamed that I hadn't managed things better.
- I wouldn't be able to pay for the room I had rented from the neighbors, and my kids and I would end up living in my car.
- I wouldn't be able to pay my income taxes, and so I would surely end up in jail.
- My kids would end up separated in foster care – or worse, back with their father and his girlfriend, which would mean they wouldn't have their basic physical and emotional needs met.

- I would never see my kids because nobody would bring them to visit me in prison.
- My kids' future would be hopeless because nothing was more devastating than having a convicted criminal for a mom.
- I would be lonelier than I'd ever been in my life.

The negative and terrifying thoughts continued to haunt me, and I found that I couldn't control my anxiety. I started over drinking and under eating. I had a horrible case of dandruff for several months. I would move my head to the side and my shoulders would be covered in white, gross flakes. I didn't realize my stress was being fed by my thoughts, and that my negative thoughts were slowly destroying me.

I was alone and on my own, just as I had been my whole life. I also hadn't ever learned to make choices. I didn't know how to quit anything (which explains why it took me so long to leave Scott). I was hanging on by a hope and with a strength and stubbornness that must have developed as a result of my childhood experiences. I guess what they say "what doesn't kill you makes you stronger," is true. I didn't realize it, but I was getting stronger, but boy was it was hard.

Then something came along that changed my life. The movie "The Secret" was just what I needed.

EVERYTHING CHANGED

Throughout my life, as part of my self-studying, I have found the Bible to be full of encouragement and instruction. I learned what the Bible said about thoughts.

Proverbs 23:7 says:

"As a man <u>thinks</u> in his heart, so is he."

The book of James explains the process of asking, then acting by faith and confidence. Chapter 4: 2-3:

"You do <u>not have</u>, because you do <u>not ask</u>. You ask and do not receive, because you ask wrongly, to spend it on your passions."

Romans 12 suggests that we:

"will be transformed by renewing our mind."

Paul explained it best to me in 2 Corinthians 10: 3-6:

"For though we walk in the flesh, we are not waging war according to the flesh, for the weapons of our warfare are not of the flesh but have divine power to destroy strongholds. We destroy arguments and every lofty opinion raised against the knowledge of God and <u>take every thought captive</u> to obey Christ."

In other words, we have to fight against our own thoughts, because, according to the Bible, and to "The Secret," <u>what you think about, you bring about</u>. The more I watched and listened to "The Secret," the more I started to understand the message: <u>change your thoughts, and your life will change</u>.

Finally, I understood what the teachers of the Bible were trying to tell me – it was the universal, metaphysical Law of Attraction. I began to realize that I was afraid because I was thinking there was something to be afraid of. I analyzed what I was thinking about:

I didn't want to lose my business.
I didn't want to go to jail.
I didn't want another bankruptcy.
I didn't want to lose my kids.
I didn't want to be lonely and alone.

Ah ha!!! I'd been doing it wrong! I'd been consciously and unconsciously telling the Universe and God what I didn't want, and I kept getting more of the same. Instead, I needed to start to ask for what I wanted!

I started taming my fearful thoughts. I had to take my negative thoughts captive and banish them from my mind. I had to consciously and decisively think about and focus on what I wanted. I had to start believing that I was worthy of and deserved all the good there was. So I began training my brain to start thinking positive thoughts:

I have a wonderful life.
I am courageous.
My kids are safe and thriving.
I feel confident and at peace.

All my bills are paid.

I have more than enough money, time, and energy to have fun and pursue a wonderful life.

Eventually, I created a single, easy-to-remember positive affirmation that I posted on my mirrors, by my bed, on my car's dashboard, on my cell phone's calendar, and on my desk. This summarized my true goals and intention: *I have a happy life, a successful business, and plenty of money.*

I recited my affirmation over and over and over for years (and still do, to this day, because it sums up everything for me). I would close my eyes and visualize what my happy life looked like to me, what an ideal day at my successful business looked like, and how fun it was to go grocery shopping without a list and a calculator, or take a vacation, or hire a gardener.

When I was afraid or mad, when any limiting beliefs and thoughts started to bomb my brain, I repeated what I wanted. I focused on what I wanted.

I have a happy life, a successful business, and plenty of money.

And within a few months, everything began to change. I started to believe what I was feeding my brain. My thoughts started transitioning from lack to abundance. From failure to success. From alone and lonely to genuine relationships and connections. From homelessness to security. From incarceration to freedom. From shame to confidence.

I started to believe in myself, and to really trust in God with all my heart. I created two vision boards to help me visualize what I was moving towards. Reprogramming my thoughts was an ongoing job, and I had decades of corrupt data to overwrite.

Miracles started to happen: though I had no money for a deposit and horrible credit, my kids and I rented a warm, safe, beautiful apartment that even had a fireplace. I started dating a man who helped me gain confidence in myself, my thoughts and ideas, and my body. People I barely knew offered to help me for free in the store. I began to dig myself out of the remaining debt my ex-husband had accrued. People started purchasing my services and I started generating consistent cash flow. With the uptake of the internet and my website, and the newly created online platforms Google, Yelp, and Groupon, I started to pave a path to sustainability and success.

With my thoughts and belief in myself and the Source of all, I know I created *a happy life, a successful business, and plenty of money.*

PUTTING ON MY BIG GIRL PANTIES

I knew how to give my kids the basic food, clothing, and shelter (because that's what I received as a kid), but I still didn't know what else to do for them. I didn't know what consistent nurturing looked like. Fortunately, the best teachers were in the house! My kids taught me how to love: "Play with us, Mommy. Let's snuggle. Can you read us this book? Can we have mac and cheese again for dinner please? We love you Mommy. You're the best mommy in the world, Mommy."

According to the parenting plan my ex-husband and I agreed to, I had the kids half time – Monday and Tuesday, and every other Friday through Sunday. I cherished those times with the kids. Their love supernaturally healed much of the wounding from my childhood, and I became confident that I could learn to be a good parent by studying books and asking questions of friends and clients.

Scott opposed me at every turn and refused to co-parent. If I said the sky was blue, he would insist it was red, and then blame me for the impending nuclear winter. Asking him to do what was best for the kids resulted in him telling me that what he was doing was best, because "the public school is rotting their brains and it's none of your damn business what I do, and they're just fine and shut the hell up."

Ok then.

I knew that divorcing Scott was the right thing to do; his outbursts and physical threats would have only escalated as the kids grew up. Sadly, they still suffered a great deal of trauma because of the choices he made. Sometimes they came back to me and told me their water had been shut off because their dad hadn't paid the bill. Sometimes they recanted episodes where their dad had a fight with his wife, Jan, and that there had been violence. Sometimes they didn't get enough food.

Between my marriage to Chuck and Scott's marriage to Jan, the kids moved around a few times and went to three different elementary schools, which meant they had to make three new sets of friends. Their dad often dropped them off at elementary school as much as two hours after school started. Discussing with him the importance of on-time drop-off was futile. I tried to help them the best I knew how, and I explained to their teachers what the issue was. I felt so powerless.

This went on for several years, and I became frustrated that I couldn't legally do anything about it. He wasn't physically abusing them; but he wasn't taking care of them and was inflicting emotional abuse. Unfortunately, child protection laws aren't very protective.

The kids had to switch middle schools when it was even harder to find new friends. I knew first-hand how hard it was to make friends when you change schools, and I worried they would suffer. I encouraged them to join after-school clubs and activities as a way to make friends. Because of the different parenting styles their dad and I had, getting involved in school activities was always challenging for the kids. There was a point when they stopped wanting to be involved in activities. When they were older and able to verbalize their thinking, they explained it was because their dad always mocked their activities and would intentionally get them to the activities late, if at all.

As the kids got older and developed a better vocabulary and became more emotionally mature, they were able to explain their feelings about their experiences with their dad. In my childhood, I hadn't been taken care of and no one talked about anything meaningful, and I learned to keep everything bottled up inside. So, when my kids started sharing their experiences, my heart broke. Yet I didn't know what I could do. I was ashamed that I didn't know how to advocate for them. I listened, though, and encouraged and loved them, and I hoped my actions would help them find their voice and their courage.

To be unwanted and unloved is painful and horrible, so I tried my best to make my kids know that I loved them. I was very worried that the consistent inconsistency was going to mess them up then and later. In spite of not having parents who knew how to show me love, I have since learned that I was being a loving parent by just listening and supporting when they needed it most. I was doing the best I could.

LIVING IN THE PERFECT PRESENT

It has been over two years since my kids have spoken to their dad. He has moved out of state and has made no effort to communicate with either of them. Leah and Nate have said, "good riddance," and I agree. They love my husband Chuck, and he loves them, and that's perfect.

My kids learned to stand up to their dad, and he even sometimes listened to them. Their courage gave me courage, and I eventually stopped trying to have a relationship with my own dad. When he died a few years ago, I didn't shed a tear and honestly didn't feel a thing.

Today, my mom and I are close. A few years ago, I learned that she'd been raped by an uncle. This abuse began when she was a young girl and went on for years. The continual assault had done so much internal damage to her that she was unable to carry a child and had had several miscarriages, which was why my brother and I were adopted. This abuse explained her actions when she was raising me. She hadn't been loved or protected, so she didn't know how to love or protect. Fortunately, she learned from the teaching of different TV evangelists that what had happened to her as a child wasn't her fault. She let God remove her shame and regret, then heal her heart and soul. She has since gotten rid of her ghosts and demons. At the beautiful age of 83, she takes only one medication, and it's for her thyroid. It's been inspiring to watch her spirit miraculously heal and to see how God is restoring years in her life. I'm proud to call her my mom.

Overall, I can honestly say that we are all doing fine, just fine.

*I have a happy life, a successful business,
and plenty of money.*

And So, It Began

THE INTRODUCTION

Leah was always the freest thinker.

From the moment she could walk she was in control of her life. She picked out her own clothes and styled her hair the way she wanted. Not that I really knew how to, but she refused to let me brush or play with her hair. As a toddler, she sucked on her binky (pacifier) upside down. She hooked the handle under her nose, because that worked better for her.

She moved around our home, or the park, or the car, like an intrepid explorer in an unknown land. She had no fear, only an intense curiosity and courage. She would approach a lone child on the playground and initiate a conversation, and before long, the two were swinging and slip-sliding away like they'd been friends since birth.

Her brother Nate was nearly always by her side, observing her cues on how to live life.

When in preschool and elementary school, she always had a circle of interesting friends – and rarely were they the popular kids. Mostly, Leah befriended the girls and boys who weren't like all the others. She was fiercely loyal and protective of her friends. It was as if she'd been given a secret book on the rules to living an authentic life.

Her dad, Scott, and I had been divorced since Leah was four and Nate was two. We shared custody 50/50, and there was minimal communication and cooperation. We each had a new marriage and a new home, so the kids bounced back and forth among three different elementary schools. Thankfully, Leah and Nate adjusted well to the different school and parenting styles.

Middle school was a whole new adventure. Like most girls her age, she fell in love with celebrities, including YouTubers Dan and Phil and Troye Sivan, plus stars from her favorite TV shows, including "Supernatural"'s Jensen Ackles and Jared Padalecki. She had crushes on boys at school and kept me updated on the comings and goings of them.

Leah started sixth grade at a new middle school, so she had to make new friends. As usual, she collected a rag-tag group of kids who were unique and interesting. Some of them had issues at home, and Leah thrived on being there for them. I was grateful that she settled into the social part of a new middle school.

She made it through the first semester, but shortly into the second semester, she was miserable. The teachers were unfair and mean, she said, and when I reached out to the principal about some of the issues Leah was having, I was ignored. It was very surprising. When I reached out again, the principal insinuated that I had threatened the staff. What? I hadn't even spoken with anyone. Clearly something wasn't right here.

In the spur of a moment, I suggested to Leah that she should try homeschooling and she wholeheartedly agreed. Her dad immediately approved, which wasn't surprising, because he had never wanted the kids to go to public school. Though Nate stayed in public school, Leah started homeschooling with a curriculum picked out by Scott's wife – one that we all agreed upon. It was decided that we would all work with Leah and follow the curriculum.

She started coming to work with me on my days so that I could help her if she had questions. It was a self-guided program, and, unlike Leah, I found it really interesting. Leah followed the assignments and completed the projects, though. We talked about what she was learning, but I was no teacher, and I knew that she was getting bored and lonely.

Dutifully, she finished her sixth grade homeschool curriculum, and then announced that she never wanted to homeschool again; she had HATED it. She wanted to go back to public school. I knew her dad wouldn't approve, but we needed his approval if she was going to go back to public school. I also knew that it would do absolutely no good for me to try to discuss it with him. If Leah was going back to public school, she was going to have to convince her dad to cooperate.

I suggested she write him a letter and explain her position. She composed a letter and without showing it to

me, took it with her to give him during her time with him.
Here is the letter, exactly as she wrote it:

August 2015

Dear Abba,

Here is the truth: I am going to public school when school starts. Please don't be mad. But this is what I want, and I think you should listen and hear me out.

I need to be around people. Once every week with one or two friends is not enough. I need to be seeing people 7 hours a day, 5 days a week, at least. Even if I am continued to be homeschooled, I won't be making any new friends who share interests with me. I'm not a super-sporty person, so if I play softball or any other team sport, they won't like the same stuff as me because I don't like sports.

You say that if we are homeschooled, we would go on a lot of field trips and do a lot of sports. I believed you at first, but then I realized you couldn't take me to Hot Topic, that was 10 minutes away, when I had my own money, and you could just drop me off. You said we would do it that weekend, and as I kept asking, you still said we would go. Well, guess what: we didn't go that weekend at all, and I had to get Mom to take me.

While I was homeschooled, you guys didn't have an actual plan. We didn't follow the curriculum, we did a science project, and I wrote about seven book reports. Book reports? Seriously? I'm not in third grade, and I don't actually care if they were classics or whatever, but the reports were so bad because I thought it was boring. I read a book, took notes, and wrote a summary and answered some questions. Never changed. Jan started calling them 'summaries' after a while, but it was a book report. Anybody could figure that out. You didn't sit down and WORK with me for a whole four months. I can understand the new job, but I started homeschool in the middle of February, and you got your job in April. That's what, one and a half, two months, to work with me. You didn't.

Homeschool is NOT THE KIDS RESPONSIBILITY. IT IS NOT MY JOB TO TEACH MYSELF. YOU HAVE TO HELP, AND YOU ARE NOT. YOU SAT BACK, JAN SAT BACK, AND TOLD ME TO PUT IN EARBUDS SO I DIDN'T HEAR THE MOVIE JAN WAS WATCHING, AS IT WOULD 'DISTRACT' ME.

THE DEFINITION OF 'HOMESCHOOL' IS, AND I QUOTE, "Homeschool means a nonpublic school conducted primarily by the parent, guardian or other person who has custody of the child or nonpublic instruction provided in the child's home." CONDUCTED BY THE PARENT OR GUARDIAN. NOT THE KID. IT IS NOT MY FULL FAULT THAT I DID SO BAD IN HOMESCHOOL BECAUSE YOU DIDN'T TEACH ME ANYTHING IN THE CURRICULUM. IT IS NOT MY JOB TO MAKE SURE YOU QUIZ ME. OR TEACH ME. THAT IS YOUR JOB.

See, Mom had a plan. We signed a contract stating that if I were to pass my homeschool test in June, I would go to Vegas to see my friend. I did and that is why we are going to Vegas from the 31st-3rd. You guys did nothing to help me achieve this, and in fact, questioned why Nate wasn't going, and stated how unfair it is to everybody. It was my prize, and you could've been happy for me, because I achieved it, but instead got angry with Mom.

Why are you such dicks when I want to change and go back to public school? Nate is in public school and I want to be there too! YOU ARE NOT THE ONE BEING SCHOOLED. YOUR OPINIONS ON THE GOVERNMENT AND POLICE AND SHIT SHOULD NOT MATTER BECAUSE IT IS MY LIFE AND MY CHOICE AND YOU WENT TO SCHOOL, YOU'RE DONE WITH IT, SO WHY DOES IT MATTER??? AND I DON'T THINK YOUR OPINIONS SHOULD AFFECT MY ENTIRE FUTURE AND FUCKING EDUCATION.

(sorry to cuss, but I'm hurt, angry, and honest)

Please let me try again, it was 6th grade and some teachers said it would take until 7th grade before some kids got the hang of things. I know I can do it. I'm not a little girl anymore and I need to learn to think for myself. Please register me for 7th grade at public school. I have the paperwork we need.

I love you and I know that you love me too.
Leah

Her dad's response? "Hell no."

Leah was crazed. Angrier than angry.

"Mom, can you do something?" she pleaded.

I had to fight him – which wasn't something that had ever ended successfully. I went to the school administration, explained the situation, showed them my divorce paperwork, which clearly stated that if we, "the parents, didn't agree on where the kids go to school, then the kids will go where the mother chooses." It's sad that this phrase had to be stipulated in my divorce paperwork from years prior, right? He'd tried to take the kids out of the preschool they loved to suit his needs. But I digress...

It worked! And Leah got to start seventh grade in public school! And the angels rejoiced!

Both kids moved again to new schools, and both were excited. They immediately started forming friendships. As the fall semester went on, Leah grew more secure and happy. But after three months of school, she suddenly became grumpy, moody, and unhappy. Even rude to me, which I was not used to.

After several days of her attitude, I was sick and tired of being ignored and answered with snotty replies, and I asked, "what in the heck is wrong with you? You don't need to speak to me that way. I'm asking you a simple question."

"You wouldn't understand," she mumbled.

"How do you know? Try me."

"No way. You would freak."

I panicked. "Is it your dad? Your grades? Is someone being mean to you?"

"I can't tell you."

She walked into her room and shut the door.

This sort of behavior went on for several weeks. She continued to be moody and rude, but these times were often followed by moments of love, communication, and laughter. Two Leahs. One body.

Probably normal for a girl going through puberty, right? That's what I was telling myself. I didn't have anyone to ask, and I had blocked out my teenage years. I figured puberty was starting, and everything was changing, including her mind, her body, and her hormones.

How bad was this going to get? How long is this gonna last? She's only thirteen. Oy vey. I often thought to myself.

Leah came home from school one day very agitated and angry. When I asked her what was wrong, she insisted we talk in her room.

I followed her into her bedroom and closed the door.

I sat down on her bed. She was pacing back and forth.

"Please. Tell me what's wrong," I pleaded.

"Mom, I have something to tell you. Promise me you will just listen. OK?"

My heart started to beat so hard I was pretty sure the pulsing could be seen through my blouse.

"OK, I promise."

I held my breath, thinking that would stop my heart from beating so fast and hard.

"OK. Here goes. Mom. I'm trans."

I stopped breathing, and my mind went blank.

Then I tensed up and adrenaline started rushing through my flash frozen, scared stiff carcass. It was fight or flight time.

DANGER WILL ROBINSON!
MAYDAY! MAYDAY!
WE'RE GOING DOWN!
SHE'S BREAKING UP!
HOUSTON, WE HAVE A PROBLEM!

Seconds passed. I remember my initial thoughts were: *No, you're not. You cannot possibly know what you want, who you are, or what you're feeling. You're too young to know. This is a sin. You're too young to understand. No, you're not.*

Then my mind quieted, then the thoughts started flying.

How could she know what she wants?

Oh, wait. Remember the typewriter I asked for? I DID know what I wanted! Does she? Really?

My next thought was, *what's a trans?*

Because I honestly didn't know what she meant.

I decided to be open about my uncertainty.

"So.... what does that mean?"

She wanted to be helpful. Polite. But she was nervous and uncertain, I could tell.

"It means I'm a boy."

She paused. Smiled.

"It means I don't see myself as a girl."

Another pause.

"It means I'm your son."

I stared at her like she'd announced she was from another planet. I smiled at her, but I know my eyes were glazing over with confusion. My idea about having a teenage daughter was very different from what was happening.

I would like to say that I immediately accepted and embraced her proclamation, leaving no doubt to anyone, especially my child, that I was the textbook example of the perfect mother of this amazing sweet transgender child o' mine.

But that would, in fact, be a big, fat, hairy lie.

I am empowered to make good choices.

The Parent Game

FOLLOW THE NEW RULES

"You won't know if you've won the game until the kid's all grown up," I read in a parenting book. I was filling in the missing pieces by reading everything I could find; I had to learn how to be a good parent.

Here's an overview of what I learned: the Parent Game starts at birth. The goal is to raise a child into a productive, happy, healthy adult.

As parents, we're supposed to help our kids learn the necessary skills and lessons of life so they can fulfill their ideas and goals for their lives. We're supposed to immediately start teaching them to be independent and self-reliant, how to think for themselves, and how to make their own decisions.

We teach them how to talk, eat, drink from a sippy cup, walk, pat the bunny, read, go potty on the big potty, hold a fork, dress themselves, tie their shoes, brush their teeth, and strap themselves in the car seat. Then they get to pick what after-school activities they want to do, what friends they want to invite to their birthday party, and what to wear for their school picture.

We ask, "what do you want to be when you grow up?" and then we're supposed to spend our life directing them onto their calling. We're supposed to mentor, lead, teach, discipline, and caution. Then we should let go, stand back, and watch them fly, fly away.

We're to be there to love, encourage, build up, and support when they fall down, stub their toes, lose the game, get ignored by a friend, and get stood up by their latest crush. We are to nurse their wounds and heal their broken hearts.

Our opponent in the Parent Game is our children. Their job is to grow up. To learn, mature, try things, and experience what works and doesn't work for them. Make their own friends. Find their own jobs. Keep a budget.

Progress in the game is measured in tangible and intangibles: Are they self-confident? Do they trust themselves? Do we trust them? Are they successful? Do they have a good job? A stable relationship? A nice house in a good neighborhood? Do they have addictions? Have they been in jail? What is their credit score? Are they contributing to the national economy? Do they do their own laundry?

We do our best, right? Even if we didn't have ideal childhoods ourselves (who did?), and even if we're not ready (who is?), when we have kids, it's showtime. Our kids need us and our unconditional love and unwavering support. We want them to succeed as adults because that's how we win the Parent Game.

I was determined to win.

Yet it appears that the rules of the Parent Game have changed. Kids are more evolved in this second decade of Y2K (2000) than kids in previous years and decades and centuries. It seems like they don't want to play the Parent Game anymore. And why is this?

Around 1991, the internet became available to the public and changed the need for the Parent Game. By the time Leah was born, in 2003, the potential of the world wide web was exploding, and social media was just starting to become something. Friendster and Myspace came on the scene around Leah's birth, then Facebook launched two years later, shortly after Nate was born.

Thanks to the blessing and/or curse of the internet and social media, kids learn at an early age that they can teach themselves how to navigate life's mysteries and challenges. Tools like Google, FaceTime, YouTube, Instagram, and Twitter teach our kids everything they want to learn, and more. Their brains download incredible amounts of information and knowledge. They are learning at a faster pace than we adults can comprehend. They have already learned how to dissect and analyze the information they're downloading, and we, the dumb adults, the boomers, can't quite figure out who Alexa is and why she knows to send ads on our Facebook feed for the shoes we were just talking about with our best friend. Our kids are learning and growing without the help of us, their parents. Wait, remind me again how this Parent Game works because it's like they don't want to play with us.

Society as a whole is different today too; when I was a teenager, there weren't diagnoses such as depression, ADHD, or anxiety disorder. Mental illness wasn't something to be talked about, let alone treated. It was taboo to think or talk about, let alone act on being gay or transgender. Transvestites or "homos" were freaks, and we were taught that freaks are bad and disgusting people.

When Leah, my darling daughter, turned thirteen, she was in her groove of practicing everything I'd taught her all her life and everything she'd been learning on her own quite successfully, thankyouverymuch.

Just as I requested. While she was forming in my belly, I told her and whoever was listening that she was going to be smart, funny, kind, strong, independent, loving, a leader, a world changer, intuitive, and thoughtful. With these traits, she'd easily and effortlessly be on her way to being an outstanding adult.

When Leah announced she was transgender and explained that she was really a boy and then firmly requested that I call her *him* now and forever, I was afraid I hadn't done it right and I was going to lose the Parent Game.

Then she asked for binders (a tight girdle that goes over the chest to flatten it out), and boys' underwear, and a legal name change and corrected birth certificate, and to go on testosterone and get surgery... Well... I lost my mind and forgot everything I had been learning and practicing as an adult parent. I forgot I was supposed to be helping her learn how to grow up and fly away.

The year was 2014. I didn't know anyone who was in this situation, and I wasn't used to having anyone around to guide or help me, so I only reacted the way I knew how to. I said things like, "there's no way you're a boy. You're a girl. You're just going through puberty. Everything inside is changing. Just hang on. You'll get through this. You'll get used to these feelings and this new body. Trust me. I know. I'm your mother."

Time went on. She continued to insist that I accept her as *him*. I started calling her h-i-m – sometimes – because I thought this was a stupid phase and it would end soon.

She, I mean h-e, was adamant. H-e wanted to buy binders so h-e would feel better about h-i-s body. I reluctantly paid for one. H-e bought more with h-i-s own money.

H-e wanted to go on testosterone. I got angry, and I was scared.

"No way. Your body is developing. That's dangerous," was my response.

H-e implied suicide. I took h-i-m to counseling, where h-e found an ally who recognized me as a loving parent with mistaken thinking.

Reluctantly... eventually... I accepted what my son and my gut and heart were telling me I needed to do. I could faintly hear the Voice reassuring me.

The thoughts and feelings that I had over this eighteen-month time period were as varied as the colors of the rainbow.

But you're my darling daughter and I'll miss all those memories of the mommy/daughter experiences like getting our nails done and going shopping and giggling at funny movies and snuggling.

And I'll be sad if I can't help you pick out your Homecoming dress, your prom dress, and your wedding dress.

And I'm afraid of what people will think.

And I'm scared you won't go to Heaven.

And I'll be terrified for you at school because you'll be bullied and get beat up and the teachers will ostracize you.

And I'll be worried you won't ever get a job.

And I'll be ashamed... of you – because you're a freak... and of me – because I have thought that about you.

And I'll be angry at your dad because if he hadn't cheated on me and been so violent, then I wouldn't have gotten a divorce and broken up this family, and your childhood would have been more stable, and you wouldn't be thinking this.

This is my fault and what's going to happen if I can't fix it? If I can't fix you?

Though I don't think I ever said these thoughts out loud, they were constantly on my mind, and real enough. I was freaking out.

I eventually realized I had to transition from what I thought I was supposed to do, think, and know about being this perfect kid's parent to who and what this wonderful kid needed. I had to transition because my child's path was transitioning. I had to be flexible. I had to change my thinking, attitude, and expectations, and that what I had learned about this Parent Game was incomplete.

I learned that my love for my child had to transcend the teachings of my parents, my past, society, and the church. Jesus's words are printed in red in the Bible. His words are much more positive and uniting about our differences than what "the church" teaches. Read it for yourself. If it's a big deal to Jesus, then He talks about it a lot.

My actions needed to speak louder than my words, and I needed to *show* my child that I loved him. So, to say I loved him but then to deny the validity and importance of his experiences was inconsistent. How could I use the power of "The Secret" and change my thinking?

Ralph Waldo Emerson summed it up perfectly: "what you do speaks so loudly, I can't hear what you're saying."

I had to learn how to be there when he needed and wanted me, how to listen, how to trust that he knew what he wanted and that it was wrong, abusive, and unloving if I ignored his thoughts and plans. I had to learn to walk with him because he was on a new path, and he was scared – brave, but scared.

Eventually, I learned that by being willing to go through my own transition, he was seeing that I loved him.

And I learned how to *not* be my parents.

Through this journey, I made a lot of mistakes and did a lot of things wrong. As I transitioned, I went through the various stages of grief because my daughter was disappearing.

As a reminder, the stages of grief as discovered by Elisabeth Kübler-Ross are:

1. Denial (including shock and fear)
2. Anger
3. Bargaining
4. Depression
5. Acceptance

I definitely started in the Denial stage, and I eventually emerged into the Acceptance stage, but not before jumping around the various stages like kernels of corn in a pan of hot oil. I floated around, backtracked, revisited, and settled in the various stages of grief for various periods of time.

The next five chapters illustrate the grieving process I went through when my daughter was transitioning to being my son.

The stories you're about to read are not chronological – they don't appear in order of how things happened.

Because that's the way grief is. Grief doesn't follow a linear line.

I've included the stories that I think offer the most significant example of that part of the grief stage as I experienced it.

Once I realized that my feelings, fears, and thoughts were kind of normal and that I was moving along an almost predictable route (according to the grief stages), I felt more in control. Realizing I was grieving made it easier to accept the fact that if I was going to help my child, I needed to change.

As you go through your journey and create your own stories, you will probably jump around too. You may identify with some of these experiences I share. Maybe not. It doesn't mean you're wrong or I'm wrong. We're all different and our journeys will be different. I hope that my stories will help you travel the detour towards a different garden party than you were expecting.

When they are young, our children physically need us, so we teach them how to walk and talk and feed themselves. As they get older, our job evolves. They physically need us less but need us more emotionally and intuitively.

If what they've decided to go after is outside of our comfort zone, then we need to change. It's just the way it is. We, as parents, need to transition, right along with our children. We must become who they need us to be so we can help them on their journey. If we've set up the relationship right, they ask our opinion. They listen to our insight. They seek our approval. They need our love.

I was willing to change from who I was into who I needed to be, and because of this, I am in my child's life. We have a loving and honest relationship. We are close. He needs me. He shares with me. We laugh and spend time together.

Isn't that miraculous? How many teenagers share their lives with their parents? Not many, sadly, and I think that it's the parents who have decided to willingly let their children continue to grow and learn for themselves who get to be a part of their kids' lives.

The transition I went through helped me be a better parent to my child and has also (hopefully) ensured that my child can fulfill his destiny. Time will tell. So far so good, though.

I'm confident in my ability to win the Parent Game.

The Denial, Shock, and Fear Stage

AIN'T JUST A RIVER IN EGYPT

"So, what do you think, Mom?"

Is this for real? I wondered. Deep in my evolving brain, I thought to myself, *this trans thing is going to be a phase.*

She'd just announced to me that she was trans.

"I don't know," I fibbed. I couldn't tell her that I knew better; that I knew she would grow out of this trans thing just like she did Pet Shop Pets and celebrity crushes and hamsters. She would live happily ever after as a girl once this phase passed.

For a moment, I studied her. She had short hair that she'd dyed pink and green. Her ears were pierced, and she had simple gold posts in. She was wearing a blue and black t-shirt with three lines on it (a symbol from a Twenty One Pilots music album). Normal jeans. Normal shoes. Normal socks.

I thought back over her life. This young person had always been a happy little girl. She had boyfriends, and boy crushes, and always wore pink and was forever repositioning the clips that she'd put in her long, wavy hair.

Did I do something wrong?

Isn't this wrong?

"Mom, you're scaring me."

I was deep in my own thoughts. I had grown up in churches that taught homosexuality was a sin. And sinners were bad! I saw church leaders show unconditional hatred towards some, but not all, people who were "sinning" by cheating on their spouses, stealing, having premarital sex, or suffering from drug, alcohol, or pornography addictions. "Hate the sin, but love the sinner," was the teaching, but I saw too often that it wasn't what the church folks always practiced. I learned that you can hate certain people because of their sin. Judge them, really.

So, transgender? That had to be an even bigger sin. An abomination.

But I couldn't hate my flesh and blood, so did that make me a sinner? It's been several years since I have been associated with organized religion (that's a whole other book, my friend) because I got tired of the hypocritical dictatorships the churches I belonged to had evolved into. I read the Bible for myself, and my Voice was my teacher. Nowhere does it say in the nearly 800,000 words of the Bible to hate someone because they aren't like you. In fact, it does say, "don't judge, lest ye be judged." My take on the overall message and teaching of God and Jesus? It's "love, love, love. Just love, darn it."

I smiled at her. "I love you darling." I knew it was the right thing to say, but I think I was having a tiny, little doubt.

"To be honest, Leah, I'm having a hard time believing this. I can't understand why you would want this. Or how you know. Because you've always been a girl, and you've been happy."

"I haven't been happy," she injected. "I've been different since I was little. Don't you remember?"

I did remember, sort of. *But wasn't that because of the divorce and her crazy dad and moving schools a zillion times and having to make new friends? All that was what made her unhappy, right?*

"I don't know what to think, honestly. I know what I know – that a man and a woman are a couple. And what about the science? I mean, you're a girl. You have a girl's body. You can't be a boy."

In a calm voice, with a steady gaze into my eyes, she explained that she was born into the wrong body and that she was a boy.

The days and weeks past. I struggled. I couldn't wrap my mind and soul around the idea that my darling daughter thought she was a he.

Over and over, she explained her dysphoria – her unhappiness with her body – knowing that it wasn't right for who she knew she was.

Thoughts continued to flood my mind and soul:
When did this change happen?
How could this happen?

I was emotionally closed to her taking this next stage of her life. I wanted my child to be happy, OF COURSE, but because I am an adult, I have a built-in "I know everything about the future, and it looks glum and gloomy if you follow this course, so you best listen to me or you'll be sorry" detector that this kid was ignoring. It made me crazy.

Trans?

My daughter was not trans. No way. Couldn't be. She's too normal dammit!

I tried on the pronoun changes. H-e. H-i-m. H-i-s. S-o-n.

OK. Just words.

Then I was dealing with a whole other set of crazy and panic-inducing thoughts:

I was scared and sad for h-i-m because I was sure h-e would miss out on so much in h-i-s life now that h-e'd made this proclamation.

It was too much for me. I changed the pronouns back to what was right. HER. SHE. DAUGHTER.

A few weeks went by.

"Please call me Alex now, not Leah. Alex, your son. It's important mom."

Of course it is. To a teenager, everything is so important, until it isn't.

This is a phase.

Seriously?

Are you kidding me?

You're going to change back.

Do I really have to do this?

My recurring thoughts included: *Wait, I'm the parent. I should be telling you NO. NO CHILD. I KNOW BETTER. YOUR FUTURE WILL BE RUINED. ABSOLUTELY NOT!*

But what about those kids committing suicide because their parents weren't accepting them? It happened just last week at her school.

I didn't want that to happen.

No no no no no.

Why can't I play along?

My job and responsibility as a parent are to keep my children safe, to teach them right from wrong, to teach them to take care of themselves and make wise choices.

If this was a fluke and just a phase, then why not stop this nonsense in its tracks? Why not be all big bossy parent and make her do what I want "just because."

I've had this daughter for 13 years, and during those 13 years, NOT ONCE has she ever said, "Mom, I wish I had a penis," or "Mom, I don't feel like a girl." There had been no indication.

Did that mean it wasn't real? Maybe she didn't know how to share these thoughts with me? Or maybe she didn't realize they needed processing?

Did I really know what she was thinking or feeling that whole time? Was she just joining a fad and trying to fit in with some group of rebellious teenagers?

In my days, the form of rebellion was smoking, or being a goth, or skipping school a lot (that's what I did; my parents never knew, or if they did, they didn't bother doing anything).

I wasn't sure I could take this seriously because I'd been down this path before. I remembered when she HAD TO HAVE a copy of Dan and Phil's new book *The Amazing Book Is Not On Fire: The World of Dan and Phil*. (For those of you who don't know, Dan and Phil are Youtuber entertainers from the U.K. with millions of teenage fans and followers.) And when we finally tracked down the book, she CRIED IN THE BOOKSTORE.

I thought she was being dramatic, and it was all a bit silly. But, if I'm being transparent, it's probably exactly how I would have reacted at her age if Paul Michael Glazer and David Soul had written the book, *The Amazing Book is Not On Fire: World of Starsky and Hutch*.

So, I went along, because I was her mom, and this is how we roll and it's what we do for our daughters. But then "poof!" a few months later, Dan and Phil were dead to her.

Because that's how teenage girls roll.

That's how I was treating this whole thing. *Oh, OK, whatever, you're a b-o-y. Whateverrrrr.*

Because before that she loved the musical group Twenty One Pilots, and then there was that time when she wanted – no, HAD TO HAVE – a hamster, then a guinea pig, then an American Girl Doll.

There will be other "must haves" that she'll HAVE TO HAVE, that she'll eventually toss to the side, like she does with other things. That's what this was.

That was my attitude. And this attitude sent the message to her that I wasn't accepting or believing her, or h-i-m, or whatever. See? I kept doing it.

I didn't do it intentionally; I just hadn't put the effort into changing my pronoun for my first child Leah. Oops, my bad. Leah, oops I mean Alex, who kept getting mad and rolling h-i-s eyes when I slipped. "Mom. It's important!"

So was the American Girl Doll, and Dan and Phil, girly!

We went back and forth often, but mostly, I ignored the elephant in the room. It was a new dance: I stopped trying, he got mad, then I tried, then he was happy, then I stopped trying, then he got upset, then I was sorry, then I tried...

One morning just after he and Nate had left for school, I found a letter-size manila envelope on my bed. It was from Alex. I opened it and pulled out a one page typed letter attached to a National Geographic magazine. On the cover of the magazine was a group of people. The headline was "Gender Revolution." It was an edition dedicated to the LBGTQ community.

Oh brother.

The letter read:

Dear Mom,

Thank you so much for supporting me and my coming to terms with my gender identity. A while ago, I asked you to take me to a gender therapist. I did not have the courage to say why. But the reason why is a reason that I do not know how you'll feel about it. I have done some research on hormone therapy. It's something I would really like to at least look into, and in order to start that process, you have to see a gender therapist. The Gender Identity of Colorado has a ton of good resources that I would like to visit sometime soon. February 4th and February 11th, they have a teen group that I would like to go to. I think it is important that we consider some options for how to go about with the future of this. I want you to be with me, I do not want to go through with this alone. But I do not feel comfortable as of right now, sitting and waiting to grow up so I can do this, I'd rather at least see what we could do now. I would really like to go on testosterone, I know it will help me feel more comfortable with myself. I hope you will at least take into consideration what I'm asking for. I am open to questions you have, and I know you will have some.

I love you Mom. Thank you.
Love, your son,
Alex

I took a deep breath and shook my head. Then I quickly scanned the articles in the magazine, hemming and hawing the whole time.

I still didn't want to have any of this. But the articles showed me that Alex wasn't an anomaly. Dang it.

The letter and magazine should have made me open my eyes and made me realize that I was dragging my feet and had been burying my head in the sand, and that I should accept the fact that perhaps this wasn't just a teenage phase.

Shoulda, woulda, coulda.

Quite honestly, I was still very uncomfortable with this whole thing, and I was still blocking my feelings. I had not yet researched this whole new world. I hadn't done a web search on transgender or dysphoria, and I didn't want to. I wanted to stay in my own routine of work and housekeeping and meeting the basic needs of my kids. Just like my dear ol' dad. I was ignoring it all.

I sat down to write a letter, and here's what came out:

Dearest Leah aka Alex aka darling daughter aka child I love so much –

I wanted to let you know in writing that I love you so much and I am so proud to be your momma.

Thanks for your letter and for letting me read the articles in "National Geographic." I read all of them. The story on being a girl was the most informative for me. It reminded me how hard it is to be a girl and go through puberty. There was a statement in the article that said something like "just because you don't feel like the girls around you or who you see on tv or in magazines or even on social media doesn't mean you might be a boy."

I know you have had a hard life... it could have been easier (divorce, different schools, completely different households and parenting styles), but it could have been harder. You know you are loved, and you know that you're safe. Safe to be who you are. Safe to change your mind. Safe to try things out.

I want you to know I understand and remember how much it sucks and how hard it is to be a middle-school-aged person. Every single thing is changing, and you are not in control, and you think it will never end. I can tell you from experience it gets better. Things settle down. Please be patient with yourself.

You have always been very, very, very self-aware. You are very, very, very unique in that regard. You are probably the most intuitive person in your circle of friends. I encourage you to be OK with being alone and lonely even, because to try to fit in with people who lack the self-awareness that you have will be frustrating for you. You will find that because you just want to be "normal" and fit in, you'll hide some of your gifts, which include the self-awareness and intuitive knowing that you have. I had hoped you would be interested in meeting other intuitive people, many of whom will be older than you. Maybe you are ready to meet them? Getting around people who feel the same way YOU feel, instead of adapting your feelings to everyone around you so you will have something to talk about will be amazing. Let me know if/when you are ready. It will be amazing; trust me.

You are such a light and such an inspiration to me. You teach me so much. You are like an eighty-year-old woman full of such wisdom, but you're still only fourteen years old and going through the cruddy puberty and hormone change. Hang in there my dear. You have so many things you will do in your life, and I can't wait to walk with you down your many paths!

Love you, Mom

Alex never acknowledged my response. He knew – beyond a shadow of a doubt – that I still wasn't on board.

I know that now too.

I have good intentions and love my child.

The Anger Stage

THE LAST STRAW

My husband, Chuck, and I work together, and there isn't a day that goes by that I'm not grateful to have my best friend with me always. One day, I was especially relieved that he was right there with me. It was the day I learned Leah decided to leave her dad and move in with us full time. It was also the day that I learned something that made me want to commit murder.

I was on a phone call when Chuck stuck his head in my office door. "Leah's on the phone and she's crying," he mouthed to me.

What does she want? I asked myself, as I continued my conversation. Putting my hand over the mouthpiece, I lip synced to Chuck, "you talk to her."

Behind h-i-s back, Leah wasn't Alex. She wasn't h-i-m. She was her. Just tellin' the truth here.

Chuck disappeared, closing the door behind him. Minutes later, he barged in. "Leah is moving in with us and she's bringing Gavin."

Gavin was Leah's old beagle dog. I stared at Chuck. I could read in his eyes that the drama at Leah's dad's house must have gotten out of hand for the last time. I finished my phone call.

I had a scheduled meeting that couldn't be rearranged, so we agreed Chuck would go pick her up and also check on Nate. Was he moving in with us too?

Within twenty minutes, I was done with my client and had closed out the cash register for the day. I called Chuck to let him know I was on my way. He told me all was quiet in Scottsville, and that Nate was at a friend's house, safe and sound.

I tried to hurry through the traffic, but Denver traffic had gotten a billion times worse in the last few years. The legalization of recreational marijuana invited nearly 30,000 people to move here every month from other states. I knew at the rate I was traveling that it would take at least thirty more minutes to get to Leah. I considered calling Scott. But no; I'm still anxious around him, not knowing what he'll say to upset me, what he'll accuse me of, and how this incident will somehow be my fault. He still wasn't reasonable.

Surprisingly, I decided to call, and surprisingly, he answered.

"Hey," Scott said, civilly. "I thought you might be calling."

"Yeah, I just left work and am heading over to your house now." I was calm. He seemed calm. *Wait for the shoe to drop. Or the fertilizer to hit the ventilator.* I continued, quietly, as if I were walking on airwaves of eggshells. "So... what's going on there?"

Like a dog slobbering for a treat, Scott pounced. "Nobody here appreciates me. I do everything, and they all sit around bitching and complaining. I'm sick of this crap. If Leah wants to leave, let her. Screw her. All she does is sit in the basement smoking anyway, so what do I care if she leaves?" (Note that Scott used the female pronouns.)

I gripped the steering wheel tightly and felt my eyes bulge out. "What do you mean she's always in the basement smoking? What's she smoking?"

Scott paused. "Well, I might as well tell you because you're gonna find out anyway."

I was all ears. I pictured Leah's bedroom in the basement at Scott's house, but I couldn't image what or why Leah was smoking. Chuck and I don't smoke, and neither does Scott. His wife, Jan, smoked cigarettes, and Leah had told me how disgusting it was, so I knew she'd never smoke.

Scott continued. "She's been smoking pot for a few months now. I get it for her because I don't want her smoking crappy tainted shit. The stuff I give her is pure and healthy."

Wait, what??? Pot!!?????

I was shocked. Images of her whole life flashed before my eyes in no particular order: *when she was born; sitting on her bedroom floor reading books; getting her ears pierced at age ten; sitting in her highchair, eating spicy green chili chicken casserole, her eyes watering and loving every minute.*

Then I recall a vivid scene of her walking on a beach in California when she was barely three years old. She's wearing a little red one-piece swimsuit and her hair is in pigtails. She's far away from me, walking along the shore. Neither of us is nervous. She knows what she's doing. She's headed where she wants to go. She eventually stops and looks back over her shoulder, just making sure I'm not lost. I've never let my eyes off her since. (Take a look at the cover of this book... It is a picture of this very scene. She's heading into her future...)

I snap back to the conversation.

Scott was agitated. "She and I agreed she would tell you, but like always, she didn't do what she said she was gonna do," Scott continued to blast. "That's what I'm talking about. That's the shit I'm sick of. She doesn't do any chores. She just hides from us. And I'm sick of it..."

My mind raced as Scott babbled on and on. *This is the last straw! How could he? How could he give a fourteen-year-old pot? It didn't matter that it was legal in Colorado – it's not legal for kids to smoke pot! Is it? No way. This is typical Scott – doing whatever he wants. No regard for the law, for my parental rights, or regard for the health and safety of the kids. Oh my God!*

Scott continued, "I'm sick of this damn family! They can all go to hell. All they want me for is the money, more more more give me more!!! Bunch of a-holes!"

I stopped freaking out for a minute to laugh to myself.

What you mean, Scott, is that you realize you're married to a woman who is as lazy as you are, and if it hadn't been for her parents paying for everything, including the cars, food, the house, and clothes, not to mention cleaning the house and the cars, you'd all be living in a van down by the river, eating bugs off the windshield.

He continued to bellow his complaints as I turned down his street and approached the house. I saw Chuck's car parked outside. He was helping Leah load bags and a suitcase into the trunk.

"OK, well I'm here now Scott," and hung up on him mid-sentence.

I parked and sat for a moment, trying to figure out how I was feeling. I was angry with Leah. Shocked. Surprised. Hurt. Why would she smoke pot? She's smarter than that.

Then I remembered. My child was coming home. I jumped out of the car and hugged her tightly. "Are you OK?"

"Now I'm good, Mom."

She explained what had happened, "we were all going to the grocery store, and dad and Jen were screaming at each other in the car, and then Jen said to 'stop the car,' and she got out and slammed the door. She said she was leaving and told dad to go bleep himself. She said a really bad word, and I don't want to say it."

"Wow. That sounds scary. Are you alright?"

Her eyes started to swell with tears. "I was scared, Mom."

I wrapped my arms around her and felt her tremble with relief. Big sigh. Big breath.

Just then, Scott appeared on the front porch. Leah glared at him, then turned and climbed into Chuck's car.

"Hey Scott," I said, as I headed to the porch. "It sounds like it's been quite a day. Leah just told me about the fight in the car. I'm so sorry."

But I wasn't sorry. I hated this man. He had caused me so much trouble. He had hurt my children, and he had ruined our marriage. He was a bad man, and he was the root and cause of all his troubles. But I had to cooperate, because he was still legally Leah's and Nate's father and had 50% custody rights.

I needed to get more information about the pot.

"So, when did Leah start smoking pot?" I asked directly and calmly.

"Oh yeah, well like I said, she was supposed to tell you all this, so I guess I'll be the adult and tell the truth. She broke our pact by not telling you, so I'm not even gonna feel bad about this. She betrayed both of us," Scott ranted.

He continued, "one day she was in the bathroom upstairs, and when she came out, I could smell the worst weed ever. So, I asked her about it, and she told me she got it from her friend Zoe. You should have smelled it; it was gross. Crap, total crap. So, I point blank asked her if she was gonna keep smoking, and she didn't even hesitate a little bit and said 'probably,' so I told her that right then and there she was NEVER to smoke pot unless I gave it to her."

Scott was quite proud of the stance he had taken, but I immediately saw a few things he could have done differently:

- Like tell your thirteen-year-old child NOT to smoke pot

- Or maybe share this experience with the OTHER parent

- Or NOT BUY HER MORE POT and instead, oh, I don't know...

- Maybe GROUND her

- Maybe EDUCATE her on how and why pot is bad for a kid's brain, which is still developing and could cause all sorts of neurological problems

- Maybe not encourage it, you idiot

But that was me. And Scott and I never saw, thought, or did things the same way. EVER.

Scott kept on ranting, like he was up on a soap box. "I don't care what anyone says, marijuana should be given to anyone who wants it, anyone who needs it. People are dying of cancer and all they need is some pot and they get completely healed. But the fucking government has to control all that and the fucking pharmaceutical companies, those greedy fuckers, they don't want anyone getting better. They keep people sick so they can make billions!"

I had heard this before. Scott considered himself an anarchist, which is someone who rejects the government's control over their lives.

But anarchists don't put their kids on Medicaid like you do, Scott.

I WAS ANGRY.

Angry that I couldn't trust him to take care of our child.

Angry we couldn't co-parent.

Angry that she was putting me through this.

Angry at my parents for not teaching me a damn thing about how to be a good parent or a mom.

Angry that I felt so powerless.

Angry that the court system was what it was – that she had to be at his house during her formative years.

Angry that my parents hadn't prepared me for anything and I didn't know how to deal with this.

Angry I didn't know how to put on my big girl panties and deal with it.

Angry that my daughter was being difficult and wouldn't listen to me or believe me that she isn't trans, that she's just doing through a difficult time.

Angry that my daughter thought she was my son. Oh, for the love of God – snap out of it Leah! I've got enough to deal with!!!

I just wanted things to be different, and I wanted Scott out of the picture. I wanted him to go away completely and forever. That was me being selfish. Nate was still with Scott half time, though.

My thoughts are powerful.

Two months later, Nate showed up after school with his suitcase and two school backpacks and announced that he was going to be living with us full time now. His dear ol' dad had decided to leave everyone and move to another state with another woman. I guess he really was sick and tired of everything and everyone.

One of the best things about Nate coming to live with us full time was that he demonstrated how easy it was to accept Leah's transition. He didn't slip or struggle or hesitate. He just called Alex his brother, and that was it. He was the best teacher of all things possible during this time.

There were days Alex was happy – almost giddy – and other days when he stayed in his room and barely spoke. He was struggling, and I didn't know if it was just his age, his dysphoria (confusion about his gender), or just teenage angst. I tried to talk to him, and sometimes he would share, but most of the time, he said he didn't have anything to share.

Maybe he's reconsidering?
Maybe he's healing.
Maybe he's growing up.

I safely let go and let God do His thing.

The Bargaining Stage

HOW TO GET AWAY WITH PARENTING

Alex reminded me that Summer Band Camp registration had started. He played the trombone and had attended this camp, held on the campus of Colorado State University, last summer. It surprised me that he enjoyed it so much, because none of his friends from school went, so all the 200 plus kids who attended had been complete strangers. He wanted to go this year.

But this year, things were different. I found the online application and began filling it out.

- Name has changed.
- Gender has changed.

Uh oh. What do we do? These band geeks won't understand. I think Alex is going to have to play along with the community and put this thing away for a bit.

I took a breath and dived into it. "Alex, I think you need to stay on the girls' side this time, don't you?"

He stared at me. I couldn't read his mind. Surely, he was considering my question and realizing I was right.

Confidently, I continued, "I just think the boys will find it very uncomfortable. I mean, you're a girl on the outside. We need to be considerate of other people's feelings."

What I didn't understand was that I was being *very inconsiderate* of my child's feelings. That's the way I'd been raised. Damn that autopilot thinking.

Alex reluctantly agreed with me, and when the time for camp arrived, we headed up to Ft. Collins. The ninety-minute drive went by quickly, and I knew he was excited because he talked nearly the whole drive. I assured him that everything would be OK, and that he would have a great time.

We checked in at registration. There were kids, band leaders, instruments, and music stands everywhere. Adults and kids were clearly excited for this four-day camp. The kids came from all around the state. The format was intense: they worked day and night learning five or six classical pieces – everything from Bach to Debussy. They separated into their sections by instrument, then would come together in the afternoon and practice as a full band. There were various levels of skills and everyone was welcome. On the final afternoon of the camp, there would be a concert for the parents and other guests. To hear what this group of musicians learned in just a few short days had blown my mind last year, and I was sure this year would be no different.

Alex recognized a couple of kids from the previous summer and they exchanged smiles and words. Then we took his suitcase to his room. His roommate was in their room getting unpacked. We had agreed that he would be registered as Leah, not Alex, and when we entered the room, I introduced Leah and myself to the girl. She smiled and whispered her name, Alicia. I asked her what instrument she played, and she fluttered, "flute." I tried to break the ice between the two strangers by inquiring what grade she was in and where she went to school.

Alex gave me THE LOOK, and I realized it was time to leave. I asked him to walk me to the front door of the dorm, and we said our goodbyes. I hugged him and whispered, "I know you're going to have a great time. I love you."

"I love you too, Mom."

I was sure everything was going to be fine.

When I got back to town, I stopped at the grocery store. I'd left my phone in the car, so after I'd loaded my groceries, I heard the familiar beep indicating I had a voice message. It was from Alex. He was crying. He hated it there and wanted to come home immediately and was pleading for me to come get him right away.

My thoughts raced: *Had the roommate tried to kiss him!? Had he been attacked by the boys when they found out he was transgender!? Had the camp leaders ostracized him and kicked him out?*

I called back right away, but he didn't answer. I tried again and again. No answer. I texted, "are you OK!!?? What happened???" No answer.

Not sure what to do, I called Chuck from the parking lot and explained the situation. He told me I needed to go get Alex. I quickly drove home and unloaded the groceries. I had left my phone in the car (again), and when I got back in to leave for Ft. Collins, I heard a beep indicating I had a voice mail. It was from an unknown number.

The automated voice stated: "you have a new message, left on June 4 at 4:33 pm."

It was one minute and thirty-two seconds long.

"Karen, this is Patty Lias, with the Colorado Honor Band, and I am up here in camp, and we have worked out a solution that Alex is happy with. And he's going to stay... and this is a safe place for him to be who he is, so I don't want you to come take him, please. I hope you get this message and turn around because he doesn't want to go home. He wants to be here. And I'm gonna be happy to talk to you about all of this. I don't know what to say, but I know you have a great kid. He's just going through some things. But he's good. I want you to know he's good. He's in a room on the boys' side, by himself, that was his choice, and he had several choices. I won't tell you we've solved anything because you don't solve it, but the immediate issue has been resolved, let's put it that way. Please feel free to call me. I really hope you turn around. I just had to have time to figure this out, and we have. Thank you. Bye."

I started crying, realizing I'd blown it. Again. Realizing that I'd hurt my own amazing child again, all for the sake of giving a crap about what other people thought and might feel, and hoping that maybe being with girls would remind him he is a girl. I felt convicted down to my soul. A stranger was able to meet the needs of my child when I didn't. I felt so ashamed as I dialed Alex's phone number.

His voice mail came on, and I hesitated. I wiped my nose and started to speak, "Alex..."

I burst into tears again. I continued, "I'm so sorry honey. I'm so sorry. I'm so sorry. I heard from your camp director, and she said you're happy and you want to stay, and I'm so sorry I didn't know how to do this. I love you so much, and I'm sorry..." I stopped and wiped my face again. "Call or text me when you can. Forgive me darling. I want you to have a wonderful time. I love you."

I was still a blithering fool, sitting in my car parked in the garage, sobbing like a baby, when Chuck got home from work. "I blew it Chuck. He moved over to the boys' side and he wants to stay."

"We didn't know," Chuck said softly.

"But Alex knew, and we didn't listen."

We were both quiet as Chuck helped me out of the car and into the house.

Three days later, we all headed to Ft. Collins to attend the concert and pick up Alex. I'd spoken to him several times and he assured me he was safe and happy. In our first call, the next day, I apologized again, and he forgave me for being a "douche." His word. I couldn't disagree.

The other conversations were as deep and meaningful as could be expected, considering he was in his happy place, on a college campus, with his people, far, far away from parents.

Alex: "Hi."

Me: "Hello!!! Are ya having fun?"

Alex: "Yeah! Loads. I gotta go."

Me: "OK. See you soon. Love you--"

CLICK.

When we arrived, we went straight to the concert hall. The musicians were scattered everywhere, taking pictures, warming up, laughing, and having fun. They were all wearing their standard uniform: Summer Camp Honor Band t-shirts and black pants. They had bonded quickly, and I was so excited to find Alex.

We found the trombones and other low brass musicians in a corner of the hall. They were sitting in a circle, facing one another, and playing Uno. Their instruments were strewn around them. Alex didn't see us, but we saw him. He was smiling and joking with everyone. There were sparkles in his eyes that I hadn't seen in a long while. My eyes started to swell with tears and at that moment, he looked up and saw me. We locked eyes, and he smiled, then nodded at me. "We're good Mom. Don't worry," was his message.

I was so relieved. He was so forgiving and understanding.

He loved me. He really loved me.

I was back in my happy place, with my son's heart settled safely in my heart.

> *The right choices come to me*
> *easily and effortlessly.*

The Depression Stage

THE MOTHER/SON DANCE

Having Alex and Nate live with us full time changed everything. When I only had the kids 50% of the time, I did a lot of triage when they were with me. Sometimes they came back after being with their dad and they were visibly traumatized. They couldn't always explain what had happened, but I knew something had caused them damage somewhere. I couldn't always stick to my agenda for them. Now, I realized I had to take full responsibility; I didn't have Scott to blame for things.

I thought I was doing good. I was trying. Sort of. Sometimes. I got used to calling my child Alex, even though I would always love the other name, Leah.

Days, weeks, and months passed. I still wasn't convinced that this change was going to "take," so I dragged my feet and continued to be consistently inconsistent about the pronoun change.

We had conversations like these repeatedly:

Alex: "Call me your son. I'm a boy."

Me: "Ok, whatever, but I have a lot on my mind, and I'm too busy to change that habit overnight that I've had for fourteen years."

Alex: "Nate has accepted me. Why can't you?"

Me: "I don't want to. This isn't real. This can't be real. You've always been a girl. You're making this up. You're confused. You're just trying something new on. You're going through puberty."

Alex: "I don't see myself as a girl. I don't like my body."

Me: "No woman ever likes her body. Get over it."

Alex: "I hate being a girl, and I am a boy."

Me: "Whatever Leah."

Alex: "It's Alex, and I'm depressed. I'm not happy."

Me: "Whatever A-l-e-x. Here, take some St. John's Wart – it's a natural mood enhancer. You'll feel better."

Alex: "I'm really depressed, and I don't think I want to be here anymore."

Me: "Fine, go live with your dad full time. You'll love homeschooling."

Alex: "No, I don't want to be *here* anymore."

Me: "What is your problem Leah?"

Alex: "I hate my life!"

Me: "What the hell is wrong with your life? You've got it good here!"

Alex: "You don't understand."

Me: "I know what it's like to be a fourteen-year-old girl!"

Alex: "I'M NOT A GIRL!!!"

Me: "Whatever A-l-e-x. You can live however you want when you're on your own!"

Alex: "I'm not gonna make it that long!"

Me: "Wait."

Me: "Stop."

What?

Seriously?

Is she thinking about killing herself?

Me: "Oh my God Leah (I slipped). Seriously?"

I was screaming. Scared out of my brains. I start crying.

Me: "Oh my God Leah. Please no. Please do not do that. Please tell me."

Alex: "Mommy. Listen to me."

OK OK, wait wait wait OK. This is real? This is for real? No no no no no no. I have a daughter. My little Leah. My baby girl. What the –?

We were sitting outside on the front steps of our house. I held him in my arms, and he cried on my shoulder. Soft sobs. Deep breaths.

Alex: "Mom. Help me."

Me: "Alex, sorry, I called you Leah earlier."

Alex: "That's OK."

Me: "I don't know what to think and I don't know what to feel. This is something completely new. I don't know what to do."

Tears had started pouring out of my eyes, snot was running out of my nose, and I was gasping for air.

Me: "But you're my darling daughter. You're my baby girl! And you're a girl. You have a girl's body. And it's changing and you're freaking out because you're going through puberty."

Sob, sniffle, snort, gasp.

Me: "And what the hell do you mean you're not happy here? Are you talking about suicide? I'm sorry I haven't been supportive! I love you! Please! I can't understand why you'd want to do this."

Sob, sniffle, snort, gasp.

He was crying, too, but not for the same reasons.

He was crying because after all these many months, I still wasn't accepting him for who he is and who he was becoming, and he was tired of trying.

Then something inside me changed. I looked at Alex, and I realized that HE DID know what HE wanted. This wasn't a phase. This wasn't like the hamster and the guinea pig. This was real.

I took a deep breath, and I understood. HE was crying because I wasn't accepting HIM. I hadn't been listening to my child. I hadn't been believing my child. My child's Voice was screaming at the top of Its lungs to my Voice, and I had been ignoring everything! Through his transparency, Alex showed me how to accept his transition.

After all the months of arguing and denying, I realized I had been stubborn and close-minded. As I realized and accepted this truth, I cried even more.

I was doing what my dad did to me when I was

young. He had not listened to me. My ideas were stupid, so don't speak. Don't embarrass him with my thoughts.

Oh.

Shut.

Up.

No feelings. No opinion. No rights. Just do it his way.

Thoughts were racing inside me about ME: *do all parents do this? Crap!*

I DO NOT WANT TO BE LIKE MY FATHER!

I'd learned not to ask, because the answer was no. I'd learned not to have dreams or goals. I'd learned to hide away all my feelings and needs and emotions. I'd learned nobody cared because nobody was caring.

What other way was there to do it?

What other way was there to receive this news, that this thing that you have known for fourteen years was now completely different?

As a kid and as a teenager, I remember thinking – no, *knowing* – that my dad didn't understand. He was wrong for not believing in or respecting my dreams and desires. I've often thought to myself, when I think about that dark and lonely time, that if someone in my class had committed suicide, I would have been the next to try. I was that miserable. That unaccepted. That unloved. That unhappy.

My child has been telling me that he was that unhappy and was feeling that unaccepted and that unloved. He wants me to trust and accept.

Who am I to doubt that he knows something I don't?

That he knows a mystery I haven't learned yet? Who am I not to believe him and show him I care?

Love is an action. (Please re-read the First Corinthians verses before the table of contents. :))

I hugged him tighter, and he hugged me back.

And we rocked.

I rocked *my child* in my arms, like I had done a million times before.

Why would that change just because she is a he?

Sitting on the steps that day, many things happened supernaturally and quickly, because that's what happens when the Voices stop shouting, and you start listening.

I released and began to mourn the dreams that I didn't even know I had. Apparently, I had dreams of my little girl growing up into a beautiful young woman... going to college... being in a sorority... getting a great job... finding true love... getting engaged... shopping for her wedding dress... starting a family... giving me grandchildren who I bounced on my knee... I still don't know where these dreams came from. My soul? *The Brady Bunch? Cosmo* Magazine?

On that warm day, sitting under the beautiful sky, holding my child, I realized that I still had a child who would grow up and do all those things – all those important, significant things. Of course he'd go to college. Of course he'd get married. Of course we'd go shopping for something to wear to the wedding. Of course, of course, of course...

I breathed deeply, wiped my soggy face on my sleeve, and stared into the soul of my perfect child. God had given me the child I prayed for. Alex was smart, funny, kind, strong, independent, loving, a leader, a world changer, intuitive, and thoughtful. I had been given a great gift and the desire of my heart.

I knew what I needed to do. I needed to give him what he was asking for.

I am a good mother.

The Acceptance Stage

WHAT LOVE LOOKS LIKE

I had seen with my own eyes how unhappy and withdrawn my child was becoming, and it wasn't getting any better. I tried to get an answer about what was wrong. How could I help?

He had already told me everything; I just wasn't cooperating.

He was emotionally exhausted and didn't know what other words to use to make me understand his confusion, fear, anxiety, and frustration.

I kept telling myself and him that it was hormones. Puberty. Just hang in there. It is tough for everyone. Deep inside I knew I didn't know how to respond to my child's needs.

"I found a counselor, Mom. One who specialized in transgender kids. A few of my friends use her. She works with kids and their parents. Her office is one point five miles from your office. She charges $85 for an hour."

He was not ashamed or embarrassed that he needed help. He didn't have the ego or see anything wrong with talking to a counselor, like I guess I did. Oh! More limiting beliefs in my world that needed to expand. After all, look at my childhood. It didn't occur to me or anyone in my family or my teachers or my friends who walked home with me that there was something wrong, and it might be beneficial to get some help from a professional. Thankfully, the mental health world has evolved.

Alex didn't understand something, so he figured out what to do. He researched. He Googled. He asked around. Chatted on social media. He learned about it. He looked for help from strangers from strange lands. I admired his ability to take care of himself; I was not good at taking care of myself or for asking for help with this topic. It didn't occur to me to look around Facebook for others who might be sharing my story. I hadn't Googled much. I kept it my secret. My old school way of doing research was obsolete, and I hadn't yet felt confident enough or inclined to barge my way into the invisible, unknown cyber world of blogs and podcasts, and random communities of supposed like-minded people. I had been hurt by people, and people hadn't helped, so I wasn't interested in reaching out, because there was the fear of being mocked, ignored, or hunted. I didn't have confidence in the world, but Alex did.

"OK," I replied. "What's her number? I'll call and set up an appointment."

Alex began meeting with Beatrice weekly for an hour.

Sometimes I was a part of the session, but most of the time I was not.

Beatrice called me into the session one day.

"Alex has just shared with me that he knows you're trying harder."

I smiled at Alex, then nodded at her.

"I am trying. It's been a big adjustment," I replied.

"His anxiety isn't getting any better, though. I want to recommend some medication to help him. He is feeling very uncomfortable now that puberty is in full swing. As a person who identifies as a male, he is horrified that he continues to menstruate. If he were to go on testosterone, the periods would stop."

I stared at Beatrice.

"What he wants to ask, and what I want to recommend, is that you get him on testosterone as soon as possible."

Dumfounded.

"Uh, um, well that sounds dangerous. That sounds drastic," I finally mumbled.

This was not my thought; this was the voice of Scott, come back from the abyss.

"Dangerous mom? Really?" Alex murmured. I could feel him rolling his eyes.

I explained, "Yeah, that's not something to mess around with – I mean, you're going through changes. Your body is changing. Your emotions are changing. Adding more hormones... isn't that gonna mess everything up? Won't there be confusion in his body?"

My eyes pleaded with Beatrice: *Do not make me do this. Please drop this. Please take my side.*

Apparently, Beatrice can't read minds. She took a breath. "I'm not sure what you mean. The fact that his body is changing is exactly the point: it's moving in the wrong direction. He is a male, and his body is becoming more and more female. Testosterone will reverse and change the direction the body is moving in. It's what he wants," she concluded.

I looked at my son. A year ago, he was my daughter. *Did he really know what he wanted? What if he changed his mind? Wouldn't this cause irreversible problems? How does he know what he wants?*

Alex could read my mind and immediately responded, "Mom, I know you're scared. You are thinking about the future, like all boomers do. What if I change my mind? What if I decide I want to be a girl, right? Well, if I do, and I stop taking testosterone, and things go bad, then that is on me. I am making this decision, not you. You're not forcing me to do this. I realize there may be long term, permanent consequences, and I'm telling you that I accept them."

My eyes had filled with tears.

Alex's Voice was clearly directing his reason, and his conviction and his understanding of the situation was just, so, well, mature. Enlightened. Confident. Self-aware.

I was none of these; clearly my Voice was muted.

I'd seen his empathetic gift when he was a little girl, when he advised me with wisdom that came from Somewhere Else. His connection to God, the Heavens, Whoever, Whatever was there then. Why would I not trust It was still with him now? No wonder he was so strong.

I could imagine his dad spitting out a list of dozens of life-threatening, dangerous, horrible side effects of going on testosterone, like cancer, blindness, losing fingers, growing humps and stumps, and hair falling out in clumps. In other words, Scott would be finding the excuses to not be a caring parent.

And what would my dad say?
Oh.
Shut.
Up.

Beatrice added, "as long as he takes testosterone, his body will be activated with more male tendencies. He will lose his period, probably within sixty days. He will become moodier and maybe even angry. He will grow facial hair – maybe even a beard. His voice will change. He will probably get a small Adam's apple. And acne. His hair may get oilier. He might experience weight gain as his appetite increases. He may even sleep longer. These are all normal side effects of being on testosterone, and they are what he wants. He wants to look and feel like a male because he is a male."

"And if he stops taking testosterone?"

"Then the physiological reactions will gradually revert back."

"So, he has to take testosterone for as long as he wants to be male?"

"Yes."

"What are the other side effects, like the dangerous ones?"

"Well, there are limited studies on the long-term effects of testosterone taken by transgender males, since this is all a relatively new field, but so far, there aren't any statistically significant side effects."

"Other than I'll feel like a boy," Alex injected.

OhmyGodohmyGodohmyGod. If Scott found out about this, he would throw a holy fit. He would spin this like I'd intentionally disregarded his refusal of this treatment and would insist that we'd had long conversations where we'd agreed to not allow Alex to go on testosterone, but then I did it anyway to spite him. I could see the proverbial legal book being thrown at me. I would lose custody of my children; I would go to jail. My life would be shattered. Our lives would be ruined.

"I don't know. I have to, um, think about this. I could never get his dad's permission on this," I said to Beatrice, not wanting to face my son.

"What do we need him for? He's not even in my life! And seriously, Mom. After what he did?"

"I know, but he's still your father and legally has 50% custody, even though you're with me 100% of the time, and even though we have no idea where he is and haven't heard from him in months. I'm afraid..." I paused because I couldn't believe I believed this, but I did... "I'm afraid he'll swoop in anytime he wants and demand to see you."

"I understand what you're thinking here, Karen," Beatrice said, "but what are the chances that he'll do that? Alex said that it's been months since he's heard from his dad."

"Right. But the fact is that he *could* show up."

"Mom, you're freaking out about the future again. Let us stay here and live in the now. It's all we can control."

I didn't know how to respond.

I was dragging my feet, not because I didn't want Alex to be happy and not because I wasn't a caring parent, but because I was scared to do the right thing for my child in this situation.

What if Scott finds out? Could I put OUR child on medication without his permission, knowing full well he would be adamantly against it and react in who knows what way?

After all, when I took him to court over the whole "give a joint to your child" experience, Scott's defense in court was to deflect his obvious guilt by telling the judge that I'd been kicked out of school when I was in the eighth grade for smoking crack and shooting heroin. I was absolutely dumbstruck at the blatant lies. I was so embarrassed and shocked and ashamed that I could barely defend myself, "no, your Honor, that's not true."

Scott continued to spew other lies. Then I remembered he was a narcissistic sociopath and how else was he going to explain his illegal actions? I found a bit of strength and began interrupting him with "lie." And, "that's another lie, your Honor."

The judge ordered us to attend family counselling, since we obviously had some unresolved issues. Scott avoided any penalty for giving Leah pot. And he didn't show up for a single counseling session with us.

"Mom."

Alex brought me back to the moment, for a moment.

I continued to question. *Scott gave Alex marijuana without telling me. Was I doing the same thing? Morally, was it the right thing to let Alex go on testosterone without telling Scott? Should I, could I, let our child go on testosterone without his father's consent? Isn't that just doing what he did?*

What if I said no? No testosterone Alex. Sorry. Wait until you are 18. Because I am afraid of your dad.

Alex would... well, I knew what his option was.

He would not live in misery. He was so clear about what he wanted. He was a boy who was stuck in the body of a girl. He was already more mature and more grown up than his dad. More mature than most people I knew.

I flashed back to a moment from my childhood. I was sitting at the piano in our living room, right next to the plastic-covered sofa, my little seven-year-old fingers not at all able to reach an octave on the keyboard. I was crying. I didn't want to learn to play the piano. We didn't even listen to music in our house, so I had no concept of the beauty of classical music. I wanted to take tap dancing lessons. My dad was sitting next to me, his arms crossed. "Practice. You have fifty minutes left. Get busy." Night after night this happened. He didn't care that I was unhappy or that I didn't want to be there. He had no empathy.

>*My dad didn't care if I was happy.*
>*Oh.*
>*Shut.*
>*Up.*
>*My dad didn't love me.*

I accepted this for the first time, right there on Beatrice's couch.

I startled myself back from the past and remembered I was in Beatrice's office. I looked at Alex, who was staring at me with a look of confusion. I was sobbing, tears and snot running full steam ahead out of my eyes and nose. I sensed something changing inside of me. I felt the blood begin to surge through my body. I heard the loud beating of my heart. The hair on my arms and back of my neck stood up. I was sweating, but I also felt a shiver go down my spine. The ticking of the clock on the coffee table made the walls vibrate.

>*I want to be a different parent than my dad.*
>*I care about my child's happiness.*
>*I love my son.*
>*It's time for my own transition.*

At this precise moment, I intentionally and finally pushed out the fear and suppression that had been plaguing me. I threw off the suit of indifference and unlove thrown on me by my dad, the church, and society, then buckled tightly by Scott. I released this restrictive mindset and attitude that had always kept me from taking responsibility and standing up for myself and my children.

This was the moment when I changed.

This was the moment when I realized that for too long, I had been behaving as a powerless victim.

This was the moment when I decided that from now on, I was going to be a strong woman and empowered mother, and that I could and would make the right decisions to ensure happiness for my child and myself. And that I would defend my rights and the rights of my children no matter who disagreed.

I will no longer follow your rules. You don't scare me anymore. I will no longer Oh. Shut. Up.

I sat up straight and looked at Beatrice first, then I stared deeply into Alex's eyes. With a power and a confidence that had been hidden deep down inside me, I announced firmly, "You're absolutely right. He has no control over us anymore. He has no say. We're doing it."

Alex's bright eyes and full smile told me it was a moment he had been hoping for since the beginning. Beatrice smiled and nodded with approval.

I had cut the invisible cord to my past, to the two men and all the others who had stopped me from living my authentic self. I no longer cared what they thought – or really, what anyone might think. I was putting on my big girl panties and doing the right thing for my child.

I was a new creation.

I easily and gracefully transcend limiting boundaries.

New Words, New Ways

HOMECOMING

It had started with the pronouns. He instead of she. Him instead of her. Son instead of daughter.

Then it moved to the name change. It used to be Leah. Now it was Alex – legally, including the social security card, birth certificate, and driver's license.

Then the testosterone appointments, and the self-administered injections.

Happy boy. No more girl.

As we matured, we were very accepting of each other's changes.

He had known what he wanted, and as he learned the way to talk with me, I realized how scared he had been to tell me.

I learned I had to get over my fears, insecurities, mental blocks, and anxieties. I had to transition, and he had a lot to teach me.

With each conversation I was more and more inspired by his ability to articulate what he wanted.

When he came out to me as transgender, he had

been very concerned that I was going to reject him. This had happened to his friends at school and on social media – some of them got kicked out of their houses. Other friends found that one or both of their parents just stopped speaking to them.

I had gone through phases where I had forgotten the rules of the Parent Game (love, nurture, care, grow, fly, fly away). I wanted to control, restrict, and shut down original thoughts and ideas. No, Child of Mine, Do It MY Way. Do What I Say. That may have worked when I was a teenager, but not with today's teenagers. And not with Alex's old soul.

There was the concern about suicide. One year, in his school district, there were three suicides and four suicide attempts by kids who were not accepted as their true identity. Thankfully, he was in a very accepting school, so I could not imagine what the suicide rate would have been if the school district had not been accepting. My way or the highway? Kids today know about that highway. I did not want to permanently lose my child to suicide over this. No. Way. I may have lost my daughter, but I didn't want to lose my son.

I started repeating a new affirmation: "we are happy, healthy, safe, and sound."

So that meant accepting what he wanted – and rolling with it – even if it was a phase, but even if it was not – because this was my kid, my child, my love.

I began to open up, to evolve, to emerge like a butterfly coming out of its cocoon, or like a new tulip breaking through the old, dry dirt in early springtime. It was my time to bloom brightly and fly into the future. Alex taught me a whole new vocabulary. New words to me like "non-binary" which meant not strictly identifying as male or female, or "cisgender," which meant that you identify as the gender you were assigned at birth (I am cisgender). I learned lots of new words, as he discussed his new friends and their identity. In fact, he gave me a two-page chart of new words that I've included at the end of this book.

These new words were confusing. It was like learning a foreign language as an adult, where you try to correlate the English word and definition to the foreign language word, instead of just learning the word.

I didn't feel like I could learn all this. There was too much to learn.

He had one friend named Ivy who was non-binary, which meant she did not identify as either male or female specifically, who preferred the "they" and "them" pronouns, even though "they" were just one person.

One day, Alex told me Ivy wanted to come over and hang out and asked if we could pick them up.

"Them who?" I asked.

"Ivy," he replied. "They need a ride."

"Who else is coming?" I asked, very confused, because I thought only Ivy was coming.

"What? No one else; just Ivy – they need a ride."

"They who?"

"Just Ivy!" He was getting cranky.

"Who else?"

He glared. Then a dark scowl.

Groaning, he barked, "Mmmooommmm. Remember????? Ivy goes by the plural pronouns!"

It was just like Abbott and Costello's "Who's on First" comedy sketch. (If you don't know this reference, look it up on YouTube.)

I laughed out loud when I realized my error. Alex didn't think it was funny.

Adjusting, recalibrating, and transforming my thoughts, opinions, preconceived notions, and prejudices took true effort. I reminded him that I was learning everything new. I had never in my life heard of anyone who preferred to be addressed in plural pronouns, and I was having a difficult time wrapping my brain around that concept.

Eventually, a boy entered his life. A bi-sexual boy, Elijah, who happened to be Mormon, which opened a whole different can of worms in his life. We called him Eli. He was a sweet, darling, kind, nice young man, and he was still figuring things out, and he and Alex were dating. He and Alex spent time together, seemed happy, at peace, and... dare I say it?... Healthy.

Which would not be how I would describe most of the relationships I remembered from when I was in high school. Jock Joe was dating cheerleader Carol and cheating on Carol with Carol's best friend Megan. Yeah, that's the way it was.

Alex and Elijah seemed genuinely interested in each other's feelings, thoughts, personal growth, fears, and hopes.

One weekend, they were hanging out at our home, and we all sat down to dinner.

"Want some tomatoes?" Alex asked Eli.

"You say tomato. I say tomatoe. And yes please."

And they laughed and laughed.

Normal conversation, right?

We weren't having tomatoes for dinner.

I caught myself staring at them. I was trying to figure out how their relationship could possibly be working. Didn't Eli think there was something wrong here? How could he just accept the idea that this person he was with, who looked like a girl but identified as a boy, was someone he wanted to spend time with?

Eli saw the truth. Alex was a nice person. Intelligent. Articulate. Caring. Concerned. Supportive. Fun. Friendly. Genuine.

Who wouldn't want to hang out with someone like that?

Alex helped everyone, including me, be a better person. He brought out the best in people by seeing the best. By demonstrating clear headedness. He had come to terms with who he was, and he was not seeking anyone's approval. He approved of himself. He had done his research. He had figured out what was not working for him and found a solution. He did not feel shame or guilt about it. He knew he had not done anything wrong. He hadn't gotten the same crazy messages I had gotten from my parents, the church, from society, from teachers, or the neighbors who were judgmental, picky, and critical.

He knew he wanted to be happy. And he figured out what would make him happy. And he went for it.

In his mind, that didn't take courage or bravery. That was just a common sense move on his part.

How freeing would that be? To know what I needed to make me happy and then just go for it? This was being transparent. Not caring what others thought about me, how I looked, who I was, how I felt. Just being my true self and being true to myself. This was what Alex was teaching me. This was how Alex helped me in my transition.

It was hard. My preconceived ideas about what I didn't even know about ended up making it even harder on him. I wasn't supportive or understanding. I didn't take the time. I was too wrapped up in my own thoughts about how things should be, what would the neighbors think, blah, blah, blah. I had my own issues, and I had to get over them.

Who the heck cares what anyone else thinks?

Alex had already figured out he didn't care about people's opinions.

That to his own self he had to be true.

I wanted to be like Alex when I grew up.

Eli was just starting down a path of his own self-discovery, and his relationship with Alex was one that gave him courage and confidence to eventually tell his parents that he was bi-sexual. They didn't take it very well at first, or second, or third. It's getting better.

Alex and Eli dated for almost two years and to this day are still close friends. It started in freshman year; Alex was new to the LGBTQ world, new to dating a boy, and new to life in high school.

They decided to go to Homecoming together. I studied my sons for the cue on how to react: Alex, Nate, Eli, and all their friends saw two boys going to Homecoming. Perfectly natural.

Alex and I went to the department store to shop for matching ties.

Ties. Because two dudes were going to Homecoming.

We were in the boy's section, then the men's section, looking for matching or coordinating ties. As I wandered around the store, I saw the moms with their daughters looking for dresses.

In the girl's and lady's sections.

Though I had never thought I was that mom who dreamed about dress shopping for my daughter, I became very emotional and upset that I wasn't shopping for Homecoming dresses. I wasn't sure why, but I was definitely feeling something raw.

I had spent fourteen years of my life watching my little girl grow up, and here we were now, at the initiation of teenagerhood, when it really mattered to her what she was going to wear, it's not just dress up, it's a real event, a real date, where she was getting to make important decisions about what to wear, how to do her hair and makeup, how high her heels should be, how low her neckline could be, picking out matching corsages and boutonnieres, etc. It was a big deal, and I was shopping for *ties*? For my transgender *s-o-n*?

I went into the lady's dressing room and cried.

I didn't go to Homecoming when I was in high school, so I have no memories of how it should be. I had an *idea* of how it was *supposed to be*. I envisioned the storyboard from "Footloose." Pick out the date, then the dress, then practice the dance. Then I combined this story with my *other idea* of how it was *supposed to be*, and that was from any stupid Disney movie, but especially "Cinderella." The vision was complete: Prince Kevin Bacon in cowboy boots and Princess Karen in the gown, with the carriage and the slippers, the center of attention... the future Queen Karen Bacon. I wanted my own fairy godmother to magically elevate the broken girl into the princess she was deep inside. But no one ever came for me, so I had to find my own damn missing slipper, and get the horses back before they turned to mice, then clean up my own pumpkin patch.

No wonder I was disappointed and crying in the dressing room.

I didn't let him know I'd been crying. This day of shopping was about him, and I had the honor and privilege of being his fairy godmother in this moment.

Alex and Eli didn't have flowers or suits or fancy shoes. Just coordinating ties. Simple. Understated. Their way of doing things. Alex lived in The Here. The Now. The Real.

We took pictures on our front lawn before they went off to the dance. Eli had a bow tie and Alex wore a regular tie. Matching colors. They wore white shirts and black pants. Alex wore Converse sneakers and Eli wore dress shoes. They had their arms around each other's waists as we took pictures under the tree.

Their smiles were huge.

They were happy and excited and safe.

The important stuff, right?

When I was in high school in the early 1980s, that would *never have happened*. A fag, a queer, a homo... you didn't show this side of yourself in public unless you wanted a beating, severe ridicule, taunting, teasing, and shaming by your classmates, your church, the adults around you, your neighbors, and your ex-friends. This world was icky and gross and dirty.

Times have changed. Society has changed and continues to change – thankfully. Kids today are in touch with who they are. The internet has helped them figure themselves out. There are lots of labels that help them identify themselves.

Do I wish I had her back?

Do I wish I could have taken my daughter shopping for a Homecoming dress?

No, but I became aware that I wished someone would have taken me shopping for a Homecoming dress. And realizing that, and crying in the changing room, helped heal the wound I wasn't even aware was there.

I have exactly what I want and need.

We are happy, healthy, safe, and sound.

While writing my story, I asked Alex to share some memories of his experience. Here is what he wrote.

ALEX'S STORY
IN HIS OWN WORDS

I went to three different elementary schools. I don't remember much from the first few years of it, because I was young. I remember in second grade I never did homework since my dad lived so far from the school that it was two hours back and forth, so I never dedicated the little free time I had to do homework. I remember doing gymnastics for four years and never learning how to do a back handspring.

I remember in third grade I had a lot of friends who were both genders. I was a tomboy. Fifth grade was when I started catching onto my dysphoria (unhappiness about my gender) and tried to push it away by being hyper-feminine. I grew out my hair, wore skirts and skinny jeans, and hung out with girls and the few boys I had a romantic interest in.

I was not happy; cut to me being homeschooled in sixth grade.

In sixth grade, I was in school only half of the year. The first half of the year I had a C average — a C in literally every class — and had a band class with twenty people in it. I don't remember much from a day-to-day basis, but I do remember that this was the point in my life where I knew I was a guy, but I thought if I was super feminine, the feelings of dysphoria and depression would go away. They did not.

Halfway through the year, I remember saying to my mom that I wanted to kill myself. We were out on our front porch talking about something I cannot remember. But I wanted to die, I was afraid of being trans and I did not want to be. Being a girl wasn't working, the feelings didn't go away, and I didn't know what to do. But I said I wanted to die. Immediately, my mom jumped to the conclusion that the reason was due to my school not having an adequate curriculum for my gifted and talented brain (in third grade, I was designated Gifted and Talented in math, and had a decent GT program in my elementary school).

My mom, dad, and I decided I should be homeschooled, so right after my twelfth birthday, I was pulled out of school and started homeschooling. My dad had been trying to homeschool me my whole life, due to him not believing in any government involvement in anything (except his insurance, among other things. What a poser.).

All the parents (mom, dad, stepdad, and stepmom) went with a Christian-influenced curriculum. The structure of teaching was learning historical events by singing songs. There were no details whatsoever. Sure, they went over briefly each event, but since I had joined halfway through, I essentially missed half of all of history.

Keep in mind, we were Jewish. I was raised Jewish. At my mom's house, we observed Shabbat by doing Kiddush on Friday nights (though sometimes we didn't do it until Saturday or even Sunday). This is when you light candles, say some prayers and blessings over the family then have a sip of wine and some sweet bread called Challah.

I went to two different Jewish preschools and had Hebrew lessons at a reformed synagogue one night a week, so why were we using a Christian curriculum of all things? The kids learning with this curriculum met once or twice weekly at a church. I did not like any of the kids and they never talked to me. My dad saw how unhappy I was.

I was not learning anything, but worse, nobody was teaching me at home. Don't get me wrong. My mom let me study, but nobody consistently sat with me and helped me learn. Nobody taught me.

I spent a lot of time on my phone. This is where I discovered the LGBT (lesbian, gay, bi-sexual, transgender) community. I went through multiple different identities that essentially helped me slowly accept that I was not a girl. I drifted slowly and eased into identifying as a trans guy. I went from a lesbian, to a bigender bisexual, to a genderfluid (male and nonbinary identities, with mostly male days) bisexual, and finally stopped at a gay trans guy, and that's when I told my parents. I first chose the name Alex for myself and was called that among my friends at synagogue and online.

I went back to public school in seventh grade. At this point in time, I was identifying as genderfluid. I was emo (emo is a subculture, like being a punk rocker or goth); my hair was short and green, and I wore black skinny jeans. I made friends with the other emo kids, all of whom identified as something that was not cisgender. I was only out to those friends and my girlfriend at the time, who I am still close with today. I do not remember much about seventh grade; I just remember that I wanted to come out to everybody. I just did not have the courage yet.

Eighth grade. The first day of school, I was in my new math class and my teacher was taking attendance. There was a new kid in the back, and when my teacher called a name — a feminine name — he piped up in the back, correcting the teacher with a name that was not a feminine name. I turned around and realized there was another trans guy in the school, and that I was not alone.

So that's how I started. I did the same thing in my English class, and it was just fine! What was I so worried about? I told my school counselor that I was trans and wanted to go by Alex and he went ahead and emailed all my teachers. I was met with support from all of them.

That one kid in my eighth grade math class helped me have a good year, and we became friends. I had two friend groups in eighth grade, the slightly-less-emo but still either not-straight, not-cis, or neither cis or straight kids, and then my band friends, all cis guys. The group of cis guys in band did not treat me any different than each other, even though they previously knew me as a girl. They accepted me. The acceptance from my friends, teachers, and peers is what helped make eighth grade one of the better years of my life.

I thought I liked girls for a while. I thought it might be easier to come out as a lesbian rather than to come out as trans. I did not even exclusively like girls. I just had a weird relationship with being attracted to guys. I did not look like them and being with a guy would bother me since I could see all the physical differences. I never really used the word lesbian to describe myself, because I knew I was not a girl.

I remember the summer before seventh grade, where I wrapped an ace bandage around my chest and put on a t-shirt, to see it flat for the first time. I saw a glimpse of who I was meant to be. I started crying immediately; it was so relieving. (Never, ever bind with ace bandages. Since they are meant to compress, you can end up with broken ribs or other or worse damage. Do not do it.)

I came out as trans for the first time in sixth grade. It was to somebody I didn't like that much. I told her first, even though I didn't like her, because if she reacted badly, it didn't matter since she wasn't important to me, but if it went well it would give me the confidence to tell others. She reacted well and started calling me Alex and male pronouns. Since this was sixth grade and I was still homeschooled, I told my synagogue friends, and all of them accepted me. Synagogue was an escape for me because at least in that building, my chosen name was respected.

In seventh grade with my school friends, they treated me like a guy, even though nobody else did. This has been consistent; I only keep people around who respect who I am and do not leave room for anything other than that.

I told my parents I was trans in eighth grade, my dad about three months before my mom. I texted my dad I was trans before I came to his house for the weekend and told him I wanted to be called Alex. He accepted me, and the next day introduced me to someone as "my son, Alex."

After that day, however, he did not call me male pronouns or endearments because "changing your name is already so much effort." So, yeah, false acceptance.

When I told my mom, I was more scared. About a year earlier, she had gone on a rant about how being gay is a sin and how trans people are freaks and everyone is going to hell, and I had spent the past year trying to help her understand that it's not a sin, for my own good, because I knew I had to tell her. I wrote her a letter shortly after the *National Geographic* Gender Revolution edition came out. I left the letter tucked inside the magazine and told her to read the letter after I left for my dad's house. I explained in the letter that I was trans and had dysphoria. I told her what I wanted to be called. I was worried about what she would say to me. I was not worried about her kicking me out, but I was worried that she would ignore it, deflect it, or flat out deny it.

She wrote a letter in reply that I was not expecting. She said that even though I was not like other girls, it didn't mean I was a boy. That everyone going through puberty is uncomfortable in their bodies. I guess she thought I was coming out as a tomboy. The reply letter crushed my spirit because she obviously didn't understand what I was telling her. I spent the next year trying to get her to understand what I was going through.

When I had guy best friends, she saw our friendship as something that is closer to a "boyfriend and girlfriend, rather than two guy friends." I started dating a guy, and she saw that as something closer to "a boyfriend and girlfriend, not a gay couple." That guy was not gay; he was bisexual, and that further confused her. It took so much out of me mentally to have to deal with dysphoria and anxiety and people harassing me on the streets, only to have to come home and educate my mom about who I am.

I met a kid at school named Erin. Turns out that kid was trans, like me. He came over one day, and we started talking about our lives. He had come out a bit less than a year before this and had his name changed and was about to start testosterone. I told him where I was in my transition, which was not far along. I asked if his mom would be willing to talk to my mom, since his mom was not only accepting of her son but educated about what her son was going through. His mom and my mom met for lunch, and after a four-hour meeting, my mom came home (with notes!). She told me that she got it now, that I was just trying to live authentically, and that testosterone was medically necessary for me to feel comfortable. I remember that after she came home, I went to my room and cried. She finally understood who I was and had given me the okay to go on T. It still took her a while, though, to really accept and let me move forward with the testosterone shots.

My mom taught me to care for everyone and not to judge based on the surface. My dad taught me to check my sources when arguing or making a point and that I am an individual with individual thoughts and ideas, and I do not need to conform.

During the early stages of my coming out, I felt judged by my parents. Through education, arguing, crying, and writing letters, at least my mom has come around. It was not easy. I knew who I was, and I was struggling to help them understand who I was.

In their defense, they had previous expectations of me. All parents do. For my first Homecoming dance, my mom took me shopping for a white button-up, red converse high tops, and a red tie, to match my best friend's. I found out later that she cried in the dressing room, because she had always pictured shopping for fancy, overpriced dresses, and that was never going to happen.

At times, I felt guilty. I sometimes wished I had never told her, and just bottled it up until I moved away. I came out for my own good. While I felt that she deserved to know the truth, I did not want to live the next five years in a dishonest way. I wanted to go into high school with some weight lifted off my shoulders. I looked at high school as a fresh start, where I would only live as a male.

As a young kid, I've always stuck up for those who were outcasted, lonely, or bullied. I care for people. I talked to everyone. Around age eight, I started picking more of my own clothes and dressing myself more and went towards the tomboy look. I loved Pokémon, jumping on the trampoline, and riding my bike. I went to a conservative Jewish preschool. I don't remember much because, again, I was very young. Apparently one of my preschool teachers was openly gay and this was a controversial issue in my preschool. I didn't care since I was four years old and only cared about getting pushed on the swings. I've always been non-judgmental like that.

For as long as I can honestly remember, I never felt like a girl. Sure, I was feminine, but I never felt like a girl. I couldn't imagine myself growing up and being a woman. I tried to picture myself as a woman, no matter what style, and could *not* do it. I couldn't picture myself in the workforce, going by my old name, and being a woman. I definitely couldn't picture myself staying at home while my husband works, being a housewife. It kept me up at night, long before I knew I was a man.

I used to ask myself how in the hell I was going to get myself to imagine growing up and being a woman. I knew that this was more than just being a child and not wanting to grow up, it was much deeper. I couldn't even picture myself being a teenage girl. I never knew why, and that really scared me. The idea that I had to eventually grow up and be known as a woman really scared me; it felt so wrong that I would continue being gendered as female and would grow up and have that only be more apparent. I hated who I was expected to grow up and become, not just from my parents, but for myself. I saw no other option.

Once I joined social media and met people, I had my first encounter with a trans person. He lived on the east coast of the U.S. I talked with him for a few months, and he told me what being trans and having dysphoria felt like. I wondered if that was what I was experiencing. I read stories from other trans people and understood that I was experiencing gender dysphoria. I spent the next year and a half going from one gender identity to another, slowly moving away from female towards accepting myself as male. Jumping immediately to male was too much for me, and while I knew that I was male, I wanted to ease into that identity. I mean, I was a girl for the past eleven years, it was all I had known. I went from identifying as a girl, to bigender, to nonbinary, to male. That shifting not only helped me become more comfortable in my identity, but also helped me absolutely make sure that I was really trans. As I got closer and closer to finally coming out as male, I became more and more comfortable in myself.

While coming out to everyone was definitely the scariest thing I've ever done, the reason I could actually come out was because I accepted myself first. I knew I was transgender, that I was male, and I accepted that as the honest truth. If I had come out before I had come to terms with myself, or still struggled with hating my identity, I would've come off as insecure and insincere. People would have doubted me more than they did. I had to know who I was before I could let others know who I was. I was prepared to cut off friends that wouldn't accept me and would belittle me for my identity, and in some cases, I had to do that. Family was trickier, but I was prepared to educate them and to never, ever back down back into the closet. If they were just too stubborn, I minimized the time I spent with them. I could do all of this because I knew who I was, and I didn't need to change.

My dysphoria was milder in the very beginning, mainly because my voice wasn't that much higher than other eleven year old boy's. As I grew up, so did my cisgender male friends and peers, and the difference between us was more prevalent. Their voices dropped, they grew taller and stronger, and I only grew more and more feminine. My dysphoria got worse with time. I first brought up the idea of hormone replacement therapy to my dad, even before I told my mom I was trans, in early eighth grade. I asked him how he felt about letting me start testosterone once I told my mom. He shut it down immediately, saying that synthetic testosterone would give me cancer.

I asked him what medical website had that information, since I had already researched and considered every effect, good or bad, and found nothing about cancer. He said there was none, and that he just knew it would. Remember when I said my dad taught me to check my sources when making a point or having an argument? He never explicitly taught me to always do that, but I do that now due to this incident.

I started testosterone on March 21, 2019. It has easily been one of the best things I've ever done for myself. I feel connected with myself, much more than I ever have. I have no more doubts about whether I'm doing the right thing. Looking at how much happier and secure I am in the past few months is enough to only further solidify that I am male.

The best part of testosterone, besides my deeper voice and patchy facial hair, is that people are reading me as male more often. I am treated the same as a cisgender male. I have people in my life who never knew my past, they only know me as I am now. I feel understood, I feel connected, and I feel confident. I wish I could live in a way where people don't know my past, like the small number of people in my extracurriculars.

I feel like my coming out experience was pretty ideal. I only wish I had explained more what dysphoria felt like, especially in my case.

I understand what you're wondering and how you're feeling. I know you had previous expectations for your kid. Every parent does; it's part of being a parent and having kids. You daydream about their first school dance, first boyfriend or girlfriend, prom, graduation, weddings, you planned it all out without maybe even realizing. I want you to know that your kid is still the same person you knew them as. You may not have seen signs of being transgender in early childhood like my mom did. Maybe you didn't even see any signs in early adolescence. You're confused as to where this all came from, and maybe you're blaming social media, television, or kids at school for your child's identity.

If it seems like your kid is suddenly trans after following a transgender celebrity or befriending a transgender kid at school, just know that those factors are not the cause of your child's identity. Those factors are helping your kid accept themselves and grow into their identity. They are not making you kid trans. Your kid is trans. So what? That doesn't change anything you previously knew about your kid; they have only told you something that they have likely been sitting on for longer than you realize. They are just as scared — if not more — as you are. Help each other. Listen to your child, try to educate yourself, whether you watch some YouTube videos made by trans people about how they knew they were trans, or read papers made by gender psychologists about dysphoria.

If you believe your child being transgender goes against your religion: you need to reconsider what your religion is teaching you and how you and your church are interpreting it.

The foundation of Christianity is to love thy neighbor, to never judge or turn away. If your church is saying LGBT people are sick, sinners, cast away to hell, and we should treat them as sub-humans, you need to find a new church full of actual Christians. Jesus would embrace your child as they are, He would embrace their transgender identity because Jesus loved everyone, and He loved their differences. Jesus sided with the sick, the poor, the immigrants, the outcasts. He wouldn't like to see you turn away your child from acceptance in His name. What would Jesus do? (Remember the bracelets back in the day that said WWJD?)

Likewise, the Quran states that "Allah creates what He pleases," meaning your child being transgender was created in Allah's own image and vision. The Quran also says that "Allah is always ready to forgive, and He is most merciful." Allah would not create your child in His own image if it was a mistake. Allah is forgiving, and if you are worried about your child going against Allah, please remember that according to the Quran, Islam is a religion of kindness, so please be kind to your transgender child, for it is what Allah wants.

As someone who is religious, I know that reading the paragraph that applies to your religion may not be enough for you to accept your child. I plead with you to research gender dysphoria, to listen to your child, and to keep in mind the foundation of what your God would want. The message of religion is supposed to be forgiving, uniting, and non-judgmental. If you are using your religion to turn away or deny your child, you are going against your religion.

What Love Looks Like

COMPLETION

It was after midnight, and I was asleep, yet I heard the text come in. It said he'd just thrown up. He didn't ask, but I knew he needed me.

He must be nervous about the surgery, I thought to myself, as I grabbed my robe and found my slippers. *The antibiotics along with the mouth rinse must not have set right with him at this late hour.*

The light was on in the hallway, and I saw the light from under the bathroom door, which was ajar. I gently knocked, then opened the door. He was standing over the sink, rinsing his mouth.

"Are you ok?" I asked in a whisper.

He sat down on the toilet seat. "I just threw up. I think I have a fever. These are both symptoms. Do you think I should cancel?"

He was asking this question because of COVID-19, a name given to a sickness that went viral and caused an international pandemic, which had disabled the world over the previous six months. Masks, social distancing, cancelled sporting events and concerts, closed churches, empty office buildings and highways as people worked from home, half of the kids at school half of the time, restaurants with 25% indoor seating capacity or tents and heaters on the parking lots and sidewalks. Such uncertainty and so much fear. Fever and vomiting are symptoms of COVID-19, but also of the flu, a cold, fatigue, and anxiety.

I reached over and touched his forehead. It seemed a bit warm, but I didn't sense it was a fever. "You've been fine all day, and you were fine a couple of hours ago."

I continued, "it could be because it's late. And you took your medicine a little late. Maybe, you are a bit nervous about tomorrow?"

He nodded. "So nervous puking?"

I smiled and nodded. "Are you worried about tomorrow?"

"A little."

I glanced at the scars on his chest – red lines under his nipples, extending parallel across his chest. Four months ago, he would not have been caught dead being seen without a shirt on. His breasts, or excess tissue as he referred to them, were a depressing reminder to him that he wasn't in the right body. He'd worn a binder for years to mask and flatten this excess tissue.

After the Top surgery, where the surgeon removed the excess tissue (breast tissue) and repositioned his nipples, he was a new man. No longer carrying that part of a girl, he's still the same downstairs, which he accepts. Instead, he wears a silicone penis in his pants – day and night. Somehow, though, removing the breasts was enough for him, for now. He doesn't mind the scars at all, knowing they will fade. He is satisfied. Content.

Except for the wisdom teeth surgery tomorrow. He had been excited for his Top surgery, and not nervous at all, even though he took similar antibiotics the night before. Wisdom teeth are different, though. Almost everyone gets them removed. Not everyone is transgender.

As I got him some ginger to chew on and a glass of water, I thought back to when he was my little baby girl, just a newborn. Leah wouldn't fall asleep unless she was in our bed, wrapped up tightly in her pink blankie, like a little burrito, laying on my arm, snuggled right next to me. Though I cherished these times, there were also those times I cherished a shower, food, and peeing even more.

So very slowly, very deliberately, I would slide my arm from under her little neck. I would watch her eyes, praying they'd stay shut. Her cute little nostrils would flare ever slightly with each breath, signaling she was sound asleep, unaware I was trying to escape. I knew not to hurry. I would spend several minutes slowly and steadily detaching her little body from my arm, watching her eyes shift under her lids – she was dreaming of something lovely; I was sure.

I learned how to roll off the bed with Ninja-sharp

skills and make it out of the room, nary disturbing a single dust bunny or sleeping baby. Half the time I escaped undetected. Other times I was summoned back to the bed with her whimpers or cries that told me, "don't leave Mommy. Come back. I need you."

Just like tonight. He still needed me.

In four years, everything has changed: time has passed, and he's gotten older. He would've gotten older if he was a s-h-e. He was in middle school and now he is a senior in high school. He has matured, which he would have done anyway. He has gotten even more independent. More mature. Like all kids do.

He's been on testosterone for over seventeen months. He is taller than me by nearly three inches. He has an Adam's apple and is growing dark scruffy facial and chest hair. His voice is deeper. His arms and legs are covered in long hair. He has acne on his face, back, and shoulders. He is moodier and hungrier than I ever thought possible, though he's still as skinny as a stick. His facial features have changed. He is becoming more handsome every day.

The world is so much more different today than when I was in school. I had fire drills. Kids today have school shooter drills. They have "safe to tell" programs where they can anonymously report if someone is talking about shooting up a school or committing suicide. They can learn from people around the world. When their body starts changing and they start feeling weird things in their body, they go to YouTube and other social media sites and find dozens or hundreds of resources and people who will give them answers. They aren't confined to just their nearby community for friends. They find great, supportive friends across the country and around the world on social media.

There is more openness today. When I was in school, there were clear cliques and kids were judgmental and critical and miserable. There were definitely divisions. Today, most kids accept and love everyone, and they love animals and the environment. They have compassion for others. They don't care about money as much as they care about having an experience or learning something or seeing a new place. They are living their lives. They are plotting their adventures.

And now I can honestly say, "Bravo! Bravo for thinking for yourself! Bravo for not conforming just because someone tells you to. Stay out of the herd if it doesn't fit you. Write your own destiny. And harm none."

I have changed more than him, I think, and that is why he called for me tonight. Perhaps it is why we are so close, why he still confides in me, and why he is so happy.

I changed because I needed to. I fixed things in me that were broken. I healed things from my past. I restructured things about my perspective that were out of alignment, including my beliefs. I still believe in God. In fact, I have no doubt that God gave me this child and is fully aware of and in support of what has happened in our lives. Zero doubt. God doesn't make mistakes, right? I have always believed that He is in control of everything and has everything under control.

And if this is a phase, then so be it. Our kids' tastes change. Their views change. Their hormones change. So do ours. We change our minds and preferences all the time, too Change is good.

This child will always be my child. No matter his age. My child, who came from my womb, who God put there, knowing full well what was going to happen.

No matter what, I love my child. I love my son as much as I did when he was my daughter. Unconditionally. Deeply. Sincerely.

And I have a great relationship with him. We are close. We talk. We share. We trust. He's helped write this book by offering input and suggestions, as well as definitions. Thank you, darling.

What else matters? Who knows what the world is going to be in five years or twenty-five years? Who knew the world would literally shut down in 2020? Who knew there would be toilet paper hoarders, or that we wouldn't be able to go to the movies or a baseball game, and that we'd have to walk around the grocery store with a mask on? Who knew that schools would close down and kids would have classes some days of the week via computers and they wouldn't/couldn't/shouldn't see their friends, live and in person? Who knew we wouldn't be allowed to have parties and gatherings, or eat in a restaurant with our friends? If the COVID-19 pandemic hysteria has taught me anything, it's to NEVER take anything for granted and to appreciate each moment as much as I can.

My son knows how to speak up, to express his views, to defend himself, to think for himself, to make his own decisions, to weigh the consequences of his actions, and to research choices and options. I've learned to do the same thing.

In my opinion, he is not only ready for his future, he is orchestrating his future. What am I worried about? He's smart, he's funny, he's wise, he's loved, he's fun, and he's loved.

He will be fine! He will be successful! He will be happy! Even when he's down, he knows what he's doing, and he will find his way up.

Since I started writing this book, I've discovered that there are so many parents who have gone through or who are going through their own journey of their child's transition. If only I'd known you before I started my journey! But then, I wouldn't have learned what I needed to learn, and I definitely wouldn't have changed the way I needed to change.

There is more support, information, and resources available now, so many who are reading this are hopefully having a much easier time learning and adjusting than I did. I'm glad for this, as it shows that as a society we are adapting to our times. But, if you are struggling with various issues, thoughts, and fears, please remember the big picture and believe how lucky you are that you have this opportunity to be in your child's life. Do not give up on him or her or them or yourself. Be brave and face the monsters hidden away who are trying to block your transition. And even if you had the most perfect childhood and incredibly supportive parents, your role as a parent will be different. Your actions and reactions will be different, because your child is different. I have learned that most kids are more transparent than adults, so let that be a lesson to us!

Believe your kid when he says he's gay. Or sad. Or lonely. Or scared.

Support your kid when she changes everything, then changes it again.

Talk to your kid about your fears, your hopes, your insecurities.

Listen to your kid when she shares, even if it makes you uncomfortable.

Walk with your kid on the path and change what needs to change, even if it's annoying and painful.

Love your kid for who she or he is, then watch and see what happens.

Trust in God or whatever Supreme Being you believe in. You will find calm and peace sooner than later, I promise. Knowing that the same Power that holds us to this earth is the same Power that is holding your child to your heart should boggle your mind and erase any doubts that this is happening for a reason and with a divine purpose. Trust that the Source that created gravity and water and worms will hold tight to you and your child and keep you together when everything seems like it's being torn off.

You're gonna be ok. You're gonna make it. Together, you'll all be fine, just fine.

The secret to winning the Parent Game, as well as the game of life, is simple: just love, unconditionally. Love is the easiest way to win the Parent Game, as well as the game of life.

I love my family and they love me.

New Words to Learn

GLOSSARY OF TERMS

These are the words that Alex suggested I learn the definitions of, and they all helped give me a good foundation. There are even more words and meanings today, and I'm continuing to learn.

Asexual – a person who either doesn't feel sexual attraction towards people or who does not view sex as something that is important and focuses on the emotional and romantic relationship instead.

Cisgender – having a gender identity or performing in gender roles that society considers appropriate for one's sex.

Bisexual – person who has significant romantic, emotional, physical, and sexual attractions to members of both sexes.

Dysphoria – the disconnect between someone's gender and their sex.

Emo – a fan of emo, especially a person who is overly sensitive, emotional, and full of angst, or who adopts a certain style characterized by dyed black hair, tight t-shirts and skinny jeans, etc.

FTM – female-to-male. Indicates a transgender individual who was originally assigned the gender of female at birth, but has claimed a male identity through pronouns, a name change, clothing, hormones, surgery, and/or attitude changes. Also referred to as a Transman or Transgender Man.

Gay – a male whose romantic, emotional, physical, and sexual attractions are for other males.

Gender Binary – the belief that there are only two opposite and static genders and that these genders are determined by the sex assigned at birth.

Genderfluid – someone whose gender identity is fluid from day-to-day, week-to-week, etc.

Genderqueer – someone who identifies as neither a male or female, or both.

Gender Identity – how one thinks of one's own gender. This is not always contingent on the sex they were assigned at birth. There are many gender identities, including male, female, transgender, genderqueer, and more.

Gender Nonconforming – a term that refers to anyone who does not identify or is uncomfortable with their assigned gender and gender roles.

Heterosexual – a person who is emotionally, romantically, or sexually attracted or committed to members of the opposite sex.

LBGTQ+ – an acronym for "lesbian, bisexual, gay, transgender queer, and questioning."

Lesbian – a female whose romantic, emotional, physical, and sexual attractions are to other females.

MTF – male-to-female. Indicates a transgender individual who was originally assigned the gender of male at birth but has claimed a female identity through pronouns, a name change, clothing, hormones, surgery, and/or attitude changes. Also referred to as a Transwoman or Transgender Woman.

Non-binary – an umbrella term for gender identities falling outside strictly male or female.

Pansexual – an individual who is attracted to the individual person and not their sex or gender.

Queer – not heterosexual or cisgender.

Transgender – a person who feels that their gender identity is something other than their biological sex.

Resources

Resources to help you navigate your transition as a parent

Louis Hay: *You Can Heal Your Life*

Norman Vincent Peele: *The Power of Positive Thinking*

Chery Richardson: *Stand Up For Your Life*

Rhonda Byrne: *The Secret*

Dr. Karyl McBride Ph.D.: *Will I Ever Be Good Enough*

Martha Stout: *The Sociopath Next Door*

James F. Twyman: *The Moses Code*

Catherine Ponder: *The Dynamic Laws of Healing*

Google: healing, family counseling, LGBTQ

Resources to help your transitioning child

Medical practitioner: Dr. Anna Wegleitner, MD – family medicine practitioner who specializes and focuses on caring for transgender patients
https://www.centura.org/provider-search/anna-wegleitner-md

Transgender voice training:
https://www.truvoicelessons.com
https://www.coloradovoiceclinic.com

Counseling and Support: https://lgbtqcolorado.org

Support: https://www.susans.org

Counseling:
http://merkercounseling.com/counseling.html
https://www.lgbtqcolorado.org/counseling.org

General resources (legal, medical, mental):
https://www.transgendermap.com

Gender affirming surgery:
https://www.topftmsurgery.com/
https://www.denverhealth.org/services/lgbtq-services

Binders: https://www.gc2b.com

Amazon: clothing, accessories

Facebook groups for parents of LBGTQ

⊚ Just One Thing ⊚

JOURNAL THE TRANSITION

Life is a journey, not just a destination, as the saying goes. As you journey down this new path, chances are strong that your thoughts and feelings will change. Use the following prompts to record your moods, thoughts, feelings, ideas, worries, hopes, etc.

Be sure to date the entries so that you can review the evolution. These pages are intended for you to record "bite-sized" memories for you to come back to time and time again to see your multiple transformations unfold.

These questions were designed by my son and me to help you calm your mind and ease your heart.

This is your journal and your journey. You don't have to follow these suggestions. There are no rules to journaling, so make this your own. It's private. Or public. Your choice. Hide your answers or share them with your child. You are in control of this journal.

One thing I love about my child:

One thing my child loves about me:

One thing I think my child is feeling:

One thing I'm feeling:

One thing I think my child is thinking:

One thing I'm thinking:

One thing I think my child is afraid of:

One thing I'm afraid of:

One thing I want from my child:

One thing my child wants from me:

One thing I want for my child:

One thing my child wants for me:

One thing my child can do that would make me happy:

One thing I can do that would make my child happy:

One thing my child can stop doing that would make me happy:

One thing I can stop doing that would make my child happy:

One thing I want my child to know and understand:

One thing I think my child wants me to know and understand:

My purpose:

My child's purpose:

Everything else:

Karen Lander is a 50-something year old entrepreneur, author, public speaker, and business coach who started her first business when she was 14 years old. She took that hustle to start a medical spa in 2006. Karen loves using the light of cosmetic lasers and the light of the world to influence people in a positive way. Karen shares her story of building her business after a divorce that left her with two toddlers and no support of any kind to encourage people to change their lives so they can accomplish their dreams. She is married to her soul mate, Chuck, and they live in the suburbs of Denver, Colorado, with their two children. She is grateful that she and her family are happy, healthy, safe, and sound.

CPSIA information can be obtained
at www.ICGtesting.com
Printed in the USA
LVHW031501110322
713034LV00008B/849